NATIONAL GEOGRAPHIC
Reach™
Language • Literacy • Content

Program Authors

Nancy Frey

Lada Kratky

Nonie K. Lesaux

Sylvia Linan-Thompson

Deborah J. Short

Jennifer D. Turner

NATIONAL GEOGRAPHIC

Hampton-Brown

Literature Reviewers

Carmen Agra Deedy, Grace Lin, Jonda C. McNair, Anastasia Suen

Grade 1 Teacher Reviewers

Kristin Blathras
Lead Literacy Teacher
Donald Morrill Elementary School
Chicago, IL

Anna Ciani
ESL Teacher
PS 291X
Bronx, NY

Jonathan Eversoll
International Baccalaureate
Curriculum Coach
Park Center Senior High
Brooklyn Park, MN

Barbara A. Genovese-Fraracci
District Program Specialist
Hacienda La Puente Unified School District
Hacienda Heights, CA

Vanessa Gonzalez
ESL Teacher/ESL Specialist
Rhoads Elementary
Katy, TX

Leonila Izaguirre
Bilingual-ESL Director
Pharr – San Juan – Alamo Independent
School District
Pharr, TX

Myra Junyk
Literacy Consultant
Toronto, ON, Canada

Susan Mayberger
Coordinator of ESL, Migrant and
Refugee Education
Omaha Public Schools
Omaha, NE

Stephanie Savage Cantu
Bilingual Teacher
Stonewall Jackson Elementary School
Dallas, TX

Annette Torres Elias
Consultant
Plano, TX

Sonia James Upton
ELL Consultant, Title III
Kentucky Department of Education
Frankfort, KY

Acknowledgments

Grateful acknowledgment is given to the authors, artists, photographers, museums, publishers, and agents for permission to reprint copyrighted material. Every effort has been made to secure the appropriate permission. If any omissions have been made or if corrections are required, please contact the Publisher.

Cover Design and Art Direction:
Visual Asylum

Cover Illustration:
Joel Sotelo

Acknowledgments and credits continue on page 295.

The National Geographic Society
John M. Fahey, Jr., President & Chief Executive Officer
Gilbert M. Grosvenor, Chairman of the Board

National Geographic School Publishing
Hampton-Brown
www.NGSP.com

Printed in the USA.
RR Donnelley, Jefferson City, MO

ISBN: 978-0-7362-7425-8

ISBN (TX): 978-0-7362-7489-0

11 12 13 14 15 16 17 18 19

10 9 8 7 6 5 4

Contents at a Glance

Unit	Title	
1	My Family	2
2	Shoot for the Sun	66
3	To Your Front Door	132
4	Growing and Changing	200

Unit 1

My Family

(?) BIG QUESTION

What makes a family?

Social Studies
▸ Families
▸ Culture

Unit Launch Build Background Video **2**

Skills & Strategies

Language
Describe
Key Words
Identify Nouns
Plural Nouns

Literacy
Organize Ideas
Plan: Set a Purpose

Content
Families

Part 1

Families in Many Cultures . . . . Photo Book   **8**
by Heather Adamson
⊙ Comprehension Coach

The World Is Your Family . . . . Magazine Article   **25**
by Josh Thome
▯ NATIONAL GEOGRAPHIC EXCLUSIVE

Skills & Strategies

Language
Give Information
Key Words
Identify Nouns
Proper Nouns

Literacy
Setting
Plan: Preview & Predict

Content
Families

Part 2

Papá and Me . . . . Realistic Fiction   **36**
by Arthur Dorros
⊙ Comprehension Coach

Postcard to Grandpa . . . . Postcard   **57**
by Amy Tong

Writing Project: Write a Photo Essay **62**

Unit Wrap-Up **64**

 NGReach.com   Sing-with-Me MP3s ⦅**MP3**⦆ ▪ Read-with-Me MP3s ⦅**MP3**⦆ ▪ National Geographic Digital Library ▪
Interactive eEdition ▪ Games for learning ▪ My Vocabulary Notebook ▪ Online Resources

Shoot for the Sun

(?) BIG QUESTION

When is something alive?

Science
▸ Living and Nonliving Things
▸ Plant Parts

Unit Launch Build Background Interactive Resource **66**

Skills & Strategies
Language
Describe
Key Words
Sort Words
Adjectives
Literacy
Take Notes
Monitor Comprehension
Content
Living & Nonliving Things

Part 1

Are You Living? . . . . Song **72**
by Laura Purdie Salas, illustrated by Vanessa Newton ⬤ Comprehension Coach

A Straw Hat . . . . Diagram **89**
by Lily Block

Skills & Strategies
Language
Retell a Story
Key Words
Sort Words
Adjectives
Literacy
Plot
Monitor Comprehension
Content
Living & Nonliving Things

Part 2

The Daisy . . . . Folk Tale **98**
by Lada Josefa Kratky, illustrated by Vicki Wehrman ⬤ Comprehension Coach

Michael Fay and the Giant Redwoods . . . . . Notebook Entry **121**
by Gabrielle Burns
▢ NATIONAL GEOGRAPHIC EXCLUSIVE

Writing Project: Write How to Make Something **128**

Unit Wrap-Up **130**

NGReach.com   Sing-with-Me MP3s ((MP3)) ▪ Read-with-Me MP3s ((MP3)) ▪ National Geographic Digital Library ▪ Interactive eEdition ▪ Games for learning ▪ My Vocabulary Notebook ▪ Online Resources

Unit 3

To Your Front Door

(?) BIG QUESTION

How do we get what we need?

Social Studies
- ▶ Goods and Services
- ▶ Needs and Wants

Unit Launch Build Background Video 132

Skills & Strategies

Language
Express Needs & Wants
Key Words
Identify Verbs
Present Tense Verbs

Literacy
Categorize
Ask Questions

Content
Goods & Services

Part 1

Markets . . . . Social Studies Article **138**
by Cassie Mayer
⟨ Comprehension Coach

Flower Power . . . . Online Article **157**
by Stefanie Boron

▮ NATIONAL GEOGRAPHIC EXCLUSIVE

Skills & Strategies

Language
Ask Questions
Key Words
Identify Verbs
Subject-Verb Agreement

Literacy
Identify Details
Rhyme
Ask Questions

Content
Goods & Services

Part 2

Delivery . . . . Poem **166**
by Anastasia Suen, illustrated by Wade Zahares
⟨ Comprehension Coach

Money . . . . Fact Sheet **191**
by Heather Langer

Writing Project: Write a Thank You Letter 196

Unit Wrap-Up 198

 NGReach.com   Sing-with-Me MP3s ⟨⟨(MP3)⟩⟩ ▪ Read-with-Me MP3s ⟨⟨(MP3)⟩⟩ ▪ National Geographic Digital Library ▪
Interactive eEdition ▪ Games for learning ▪ My Vocabulary Notebook ▪ Online Resources

Growing and Changing

(**?**) **BIG QUESTION**

How do animals change as they grow?

Science
▸ Animal Life Cycles

Unit Launch Build Background Video **200**

Skills & Strategies
Language
Retell a Story
Key Words
Context Clues
Subject Pronouns
Literacy
Plot
Determine Importance
Content
Animal Life Cycles

Part 1

Ruby in Her Own Time . . . . Animal Fantasy **206**
by Jonathan Emmett, illustrated by Rebecca Harry ▪ Comprehension Coach

Turtles: From Eggs to Ocean . . . . Science Article **235**
by Mariana Fuentes

☐ NATIONAL GEOGRAPHIC EXCLUSIVE

Skills & Strategies
Language
Restate an Idea
Key Words
Context Clues
Possessive Words
Literacy
Main Idea & Details
Determine Importance
Content
Animal Life Cycles

Part 2

A Butterfly Is Born . . . . Science Article **246**
by Fran Downey ▪ Comprehension Coach

Caterpillar . . . . Poem **261**
by Nikki Grimes, illustrated by Javaka Steptoe

Writing Project: Write a Story **266**

Unit Wrap-Up **268**

 NGReach.com   Sing-with-Me MP3s ((**MP3**)) ▪ Read-with-Me MP3s ((**MP3**)) ▪ National Geographic Digital Library ▪ Interactive eEdition ▪ Games for learning ▪ My Vocabulary Notebook ▪ Online Resources

Genres at a Glance

Fiction

Animal Fantasy

Ruby in Her Own Time 206
Jonathan Emmett

Folk Tale

The Daisy 98
Lada Josefa Kratky

Realistic Fiction

Papá and Me 36
Arthur Dorros

Poetry

Poem

Delivery 166
Anastasia Suen

Caterpillar 261
Nikki Grimes

Song

Are You Living? 72
Laura Purdie Salas

Nonfiction

Diagram

A Straw Hat 89
Lily Block

Fact Sheet

Money 191
Heather Langer

Magazine Article

☐ **The World Is Your Family** . . . 25
Josh Thome

Photo Book

Families in Many Cultures 8
Heather Adamson

Postcard

Postcard to Grandpa 57
Amy Tong

Project Notebook

☐ **Michael Fay and the Giant Redwoods** 121
Gabrielle Burns

Science Article

☐ **Turtles: From Eggs to Ocean** 235
Mariana Fuentes

☐ **A Butterfly Is Born** 246
Fran Downey

Social Studies Article

Markets 138
Cassie Mayer

Media

Online Article

☐ **Flower Power** 157
Stefanie Boron

My Family

? BIG Question

What makes a family?

Unit at a Glance
▶ **Language:** Describe, Give Information, Social Studies Words
▶ **Literacy:** Plan: Preview, Set a Purpose, and Predict
▶ **Content:** Families

Unit
1

Share What You Know

Do It!

❶ **Draw** your family doing something together. Hang your picture in the classroom.

❷ **Act out** what your picture shows. Can your class find your picture?

❸ **Say** something about your family and the picture.

Build Background: Watch a video about family activities.
NGReach.com

Describe

Listen and sing.   *Song* (((MP3))) 💿

Our Routine

My family eats meals.

Dad's lunches are great.

Then I play outside.

I bike or I skate.

When I come home

I help Dad to clean.

Mom reads me a book.

I like our routine!

Tune: "Rock a Bye, Baby"

Key Words

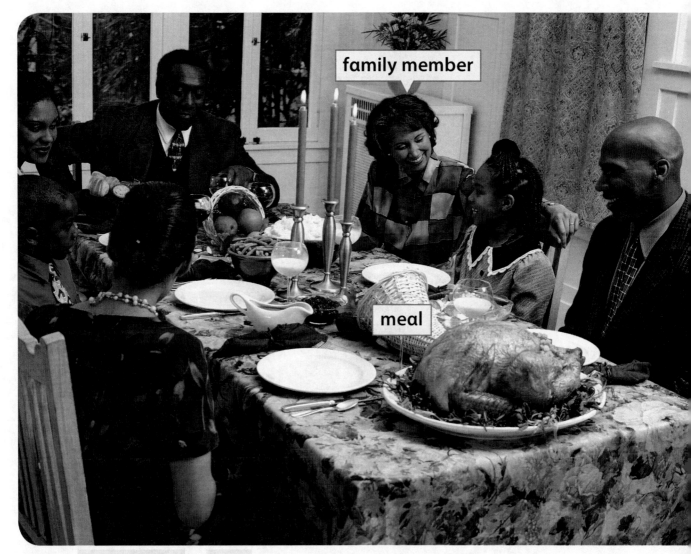

family member

meal

▲ A **family holiday** at **home**.

Talk Together

What is each family member doing? Tell your partner. Name your family members.

Organize Ideas

Idea Web

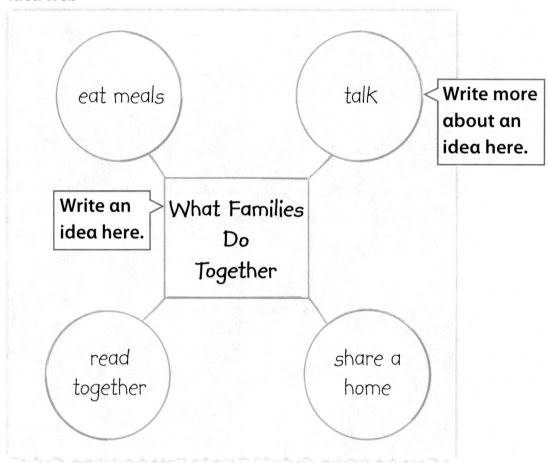

eat meals

talk

Write more about an idea here.

Write an idea here. → What Families Do Together

read together

share a home

Talk **Together**

Tell your partner what your family does. Make a new idea web. Write in the circles.

More Key Words

care

I **care** for my plant.

celebrate

We **celebrate** grandma's birthday.

• help

I **help** carry the clothes.

play

We **play** a game.

world

There are many people and places in the **world**.

Talk Together

Use one **Key Word** in a sentence.

> I celebrate when I get a good grade.

• High Frequency Word

Add words to My Vocabulary Notebook.
NGReach.com

Read a Photo Book

A **photo book** uses photos to tell about real people and things.

✓ Look for **photos**.

Think about what the photos show.

Reading Strategy

Set a purpose before you read. What do you want to learn?

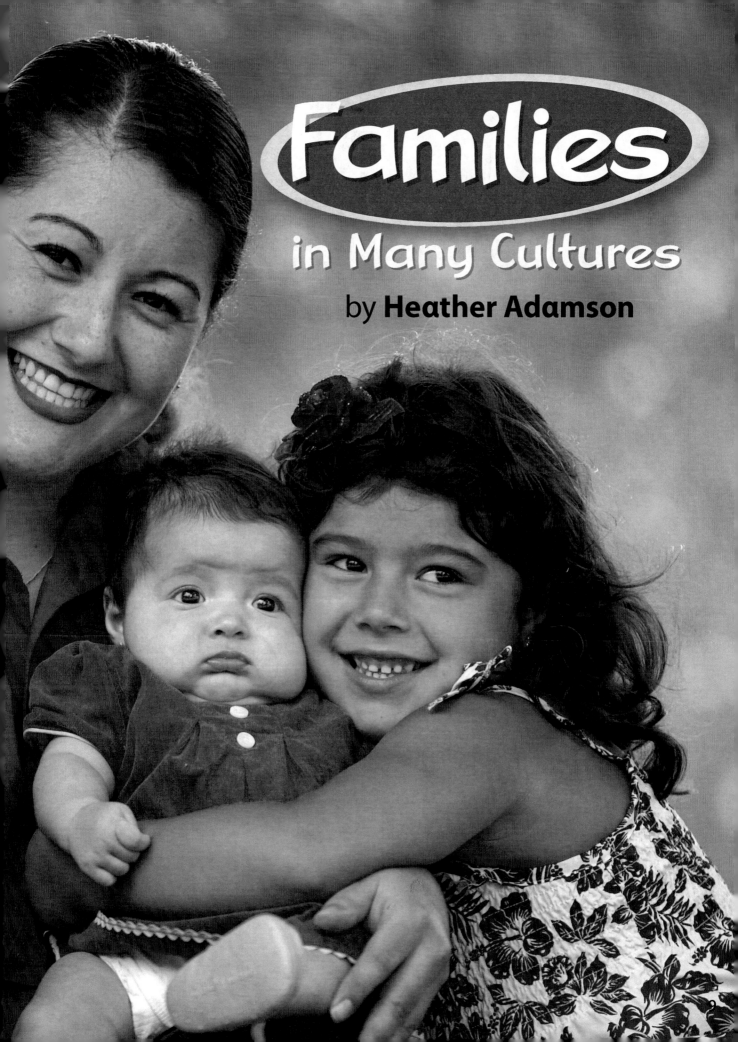

Families

in Many Cultures

by Heather Adamson

Families of all sizes

live around the **world**.

Families help

each other.

Families

share **meals**.

Families **celebrate** **holidays**.

Families celebrate birthdays.

Families **play** together.

Families laugh together.

What is your family like? ❖

Talk About It

1. What do **families** **celebrate**?

   Families celebrate _____ .

2. How are some families the same?

   Some families _____ .

3. What purpose did you set for reading?
   What did you learn?

   I wanted to learn _____ .
   I learned _____ .

Learn test-taking strategies.
⊘ NGReach.com

Write About It

How does your family **help** you?

My family helps me _____ .

Organize Ideas

What do the families in the story do together?

Idea Web

Use your web. Tell a partner what you learned in "Families in Many Cultures".

> The families celebrate birthdays.

23

Identify Nouns

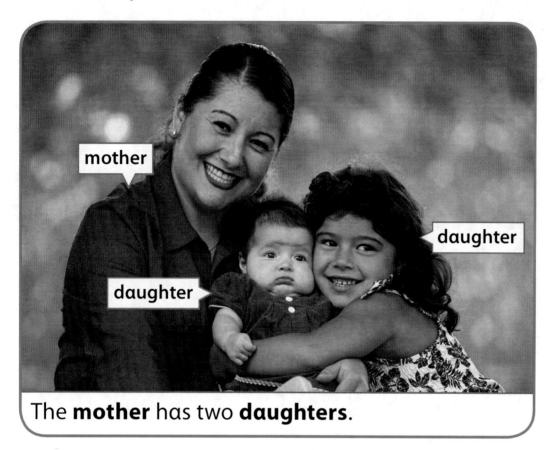

mother

daughter

daughter

The **mother** has two **daughters**.

A **noun** names a person or people.

Try It Together

Read the list of words. Draw a
picture to show each noun.
How are the nouns alike?

Nouns
man
baby
sister
teachers

Connect Across Texts Learn more about what makes a **family**.

Genre A **magazine article** is nonfiction. It often tells about something going on in the **world** now.

The World Is Your Family

by Josh Thome

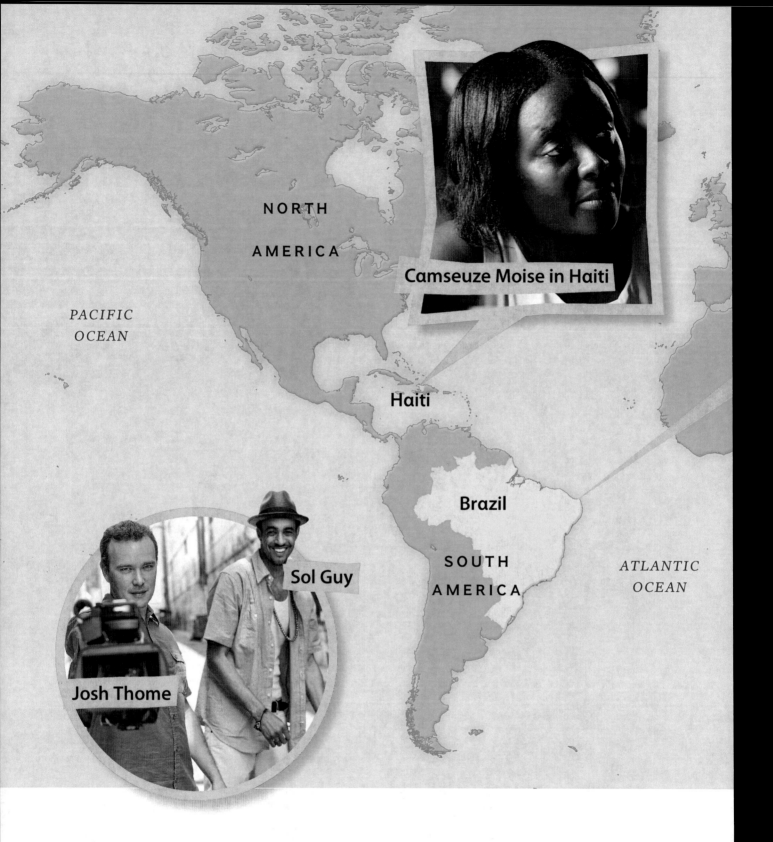

Camseuze Moise in Haiti

Haiti

Brazil

Sol Guy

Josh Thome

NORTH AMERICA

SOUTH AMERICA

PACIFIC OCEAN

ATLANTIC OCEAN

We meet people all over the world.

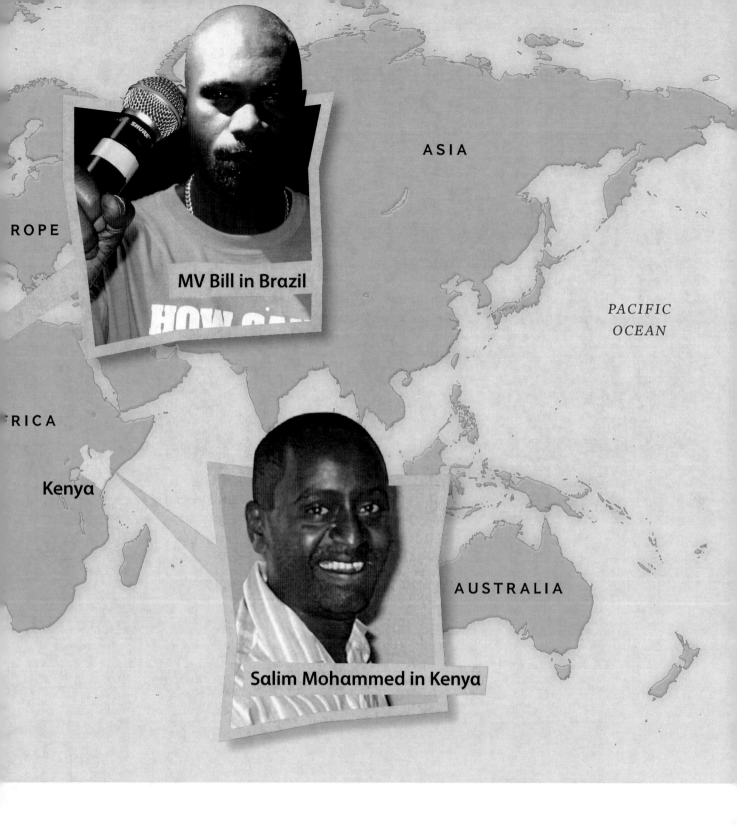

ASIA

PACIFIC
OCEAN

ROPE

MV Bill in Brazil

RICA

Kenya

AUSTRALIA

Salim Mohammed in Kenya

These people **help** others.

Salim Mohammed has a sports program to help kids.

Camseuze Moise teaches about health all over Haiti.

Their message is important.

Singer MV Bill built a community center.

Be family to the world around you.

Compare Author's Purpose

Authors have different purposes for writing.

"Families in Many Cultures"

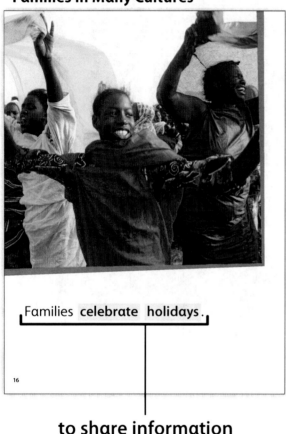

Families celebrate holidays.

16

to share information

"The World Is Your Family"

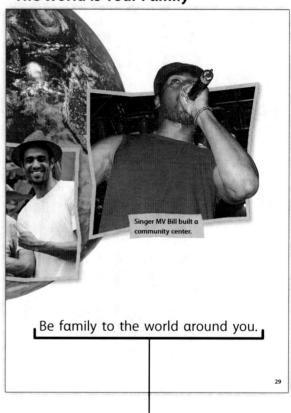

Singer MV Bill built a community center.

Be family to the world around you.

29

to tell you what they think

Tell another purpose the authors had for writing their texts.

Talk Together

Think about what you read and learned. What makes a family?

Plural Nouns

A **noun** names one person, place, or thing.

 box   home

A **plural noun** names more than one.

 boxes   homes

Grammar Rules **Plural Nouns**

Add **s** to most nouns to show more than one.	Add **es** to nouns that end in **ss**, **x**, **ch**, and **sh** to show more than one.

Read a Sentence

Why do the nouns have **s** or **es**?

We had **sandwiches** for our **meals**.

Write a Sentence

Write a sentence to tell about one of your family's meals. Use a plural noun. Read it to a partner.

Give Information

Listen and sing.　***Song*** (((MP3)))

I go to Dawes Pool.

This is where I play.

I am with my family.

I have fun today.

I go to Oz Park.

This is where I cheer.

I am with my family.

All the fans are here.

Tune: "Row, Row, Row Your Boat"

Key Words

Family Photos

This was a **special** day. My **parents** and I saw a parade **together**. It was **fun**!

This is my **extended family**. We **visit** them every year. That is fun, too!

Talk Together

Look at the family photo book. Where do they go? Where do you go with your family?

Identify Setting

Setting Chart

Movie Theater	Picture of the Place
• dark • big • many seats	

^ Write about a place here.

^ Draw the place here.

Talk Together

Make a setting chart about a family story you know. Share it with your partner.

More Key Words

group

A **group** has more than two items.

idea

Lori's **idea** is to go to the zoo.

place

The school is a big **place**.

share

We **share** popcorn.

trip

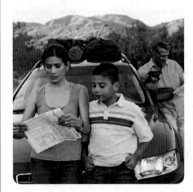

We take a **trip** in our car.

Talk Together

Count the syllables in **Key Words**.

> Group has one syllable. Idea has three.

Add words to My Vocabulary Notebook.
NGReach.com

Read a Story

Where does this story happen?

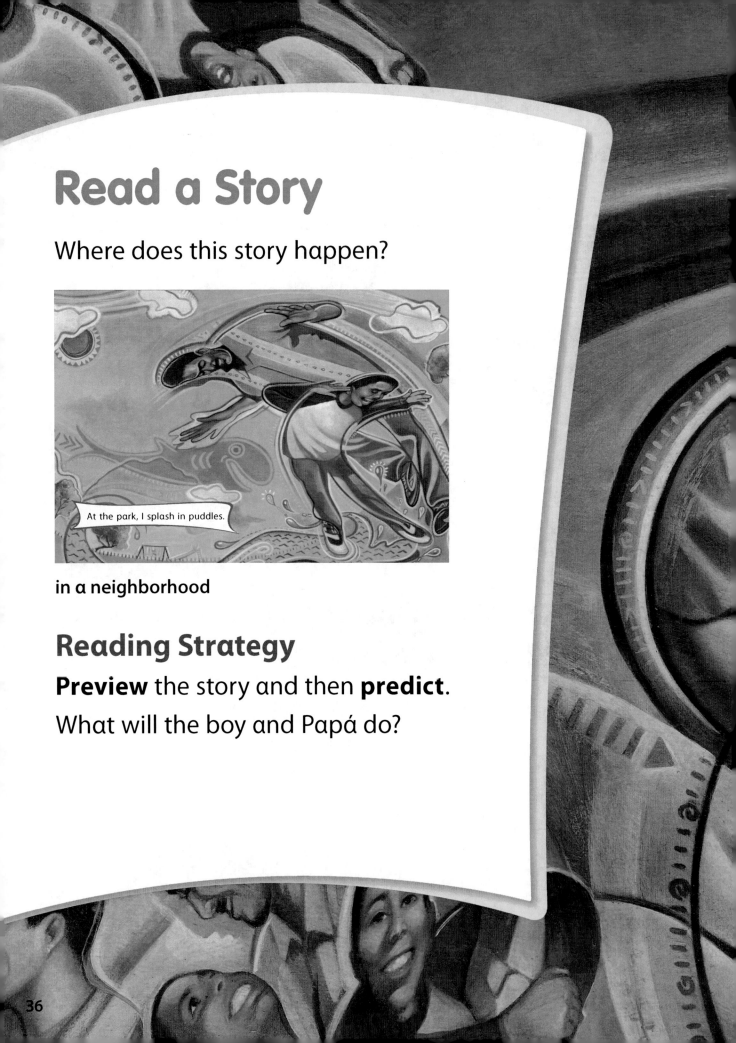

At the park, I splash in puddles.

in a neighborhood

Reading Strategy

Preview the story and then **predict**.

What will the boy and Papá do?

Papá and Me

by **Arthur Dorros**

Good morning, Papá!

It will be a **fun** day.

We cook something new.

We walk. We hold hands.

At the park, I splash in puddles.

Papá lifts me.

Papá draws my face.

I draw his face.

We **share** stories on the bus.

My grandparents hug
Papá and me. ❖

Meet the Author

Arthur Dorros

AWARD WINNER

Arthur Dorros loved to read books when he was a boy. Now he loves to write books!

Mr. Dorros thinks he is very lucky. He grew up with a great dad. Now he has a great son. That is why he wrote *Papá and Me*.

▲ Arthur Dorros

Writer's Craft

In *Papá and Me*, the author shares details about the characters' day together. Write a sentence about one of the characters.

Talk About It

1. What do Papá and the boy do at home?

At home, they ___ .

2. How can you tell they love each other?

They ___ and ___ .

3. What did you predict they would do? Did your prediction happen?

I predicted they would ___ .
My prediction ___ .

Write About It

How do you have **fun** with your family?

We like to ___ together.

54

Identify Setting

Where do Papá and his son go? What are the **places** like? Write words or draw.

Setting Chart

Places	What the Places are Like
• home	• fun
•	•
•	•

Use your chart. Give information about the places in *Papá and Me.*

They go to the park.

Identify Nouns

Nouns

At the **park**, I splash in puddles.

A **noun** names a place.

Read the list of words. Which ones are nouns? How do you know?

go
home
library
play

Postcard to Grandpa

by Amy Tong

Greetings from ARIZONA

March 15

Dear Grandpa,

　　Arizona is so **fun**. I like

riding the horses. You should

come to this **place**.

We miss you!

Love,

Amy

Arizona

To: <u>Grandpa Tong</u>

<u>820 Sunnybrook</u>

<u>Greenhill, Wisconsin 93759</u>

Compare Genres

How are *Papá and Me* and "Postcard to Grandparents" different?

Realistic Fiction

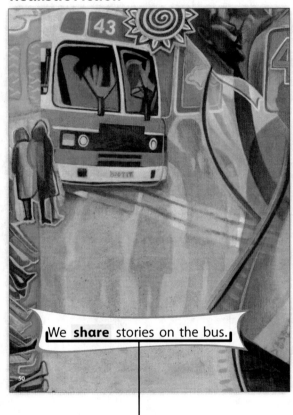

We **share** stories on the bus.

50

The story is made up, but it seems real.

Postcard

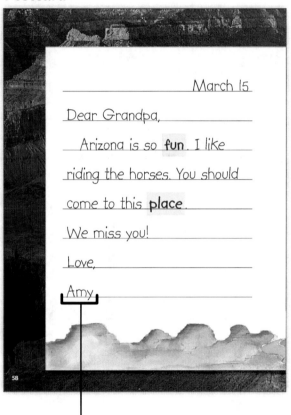

March 15

Dear Grandpa,

   Arizona is so **fun**. I like riding the horses. You should come to this **place**.

We miss you!

Love,

Amy

58

The postcard is a message from a real person.

Talk Together

Think about what you read and learned. What makes a family?

Proper Nouns

A **proper noun** is the name of a special person, animal, or place.

I see **Amy**.

Grammar Rules Proper Nouns	
Start a **proper noun** with a capital letter.	My grandpa likes his dog **B**o.
	capital letter
	Grandpa walks on **C**herry **S**treet.
	capital letters

Read a Sentence

Why does Chávez Park have capital letters?

Papá and I went to Chávez Park.

Write Sentences

Write a sentence about a family member. Use the name of your family member in the sentence. Read it to a partner.

Write as a Family Member

Write a Photo Essay

Where does your family go? Tell about a special place. Write a photo essay for your family.

Our Family Place

by Bali Rashidi

We go to Camp Blue Lake.

A photo essay has photos.

Captions give information about the photos, like the **setting** or people pictured.

This is where we cook outside.

Language Frames
• We go to _____ .
• This is where _____ .

❶ Plan and Write

Work with a partner. Talk about places you go with your family. Pick one place. Find photos or make drawings of the place. Tell your partner about the place.

Write about where you go. Then write about why the place is special. Match each sentence with a picture.

❷ Check Your Work

Revise and edit your writing. Use this checklist.

Checklist

☑ Think about different nouns you can use. Can you use nouns that name people and places?

☑ Check your sentences. Did you begin names of special places with a capital letter?

☑ Read each line of your work. Keep track of words you misspell. Make your own spelling list.

❸ Finish and Share

Finish your photo essay. Write each sentence neatly. Leave space between words.

Read your photo essay aloud. Hold up the photos so that the group can see. Sit quietly while others speak. Share what you know.

I have fun with my family!

63

Share Your Ideas

Think about the things families do
together. What makes a family? Choose
one of these ways to share your ideas
about the **Big Question**.

Write It!

Draw a Chart

Work together to make a chart.
Write the title **Family Sizes**.
Write your names on the left.
Draw the number of people
in your family on the right.
Compare family sizes.

Family Sizes

James

Marta

Talk About It!

Plan a Family Trip

As a group, plan a great family trip. Make a list of where you would go, what you would do there, and how you would get there. Locate the places on a map.

We would take a train.

Do It!

My Helping Hands

Trace your hands on a piece of paper. Write one way you help out at home on each finger.

I feed my cat.

Shoot for the Sun

? BIG Question

When is something alive?

Unit at a Glance
▸ **Language**: Describe, Retell a Story, Science Words
▸ **Literacy:** Monitor
▸ **Content**: Living and Nonliving Things

Unit
2

Share What You Know

Do It!

❶ **Think** of something that is alive.

❷ **Act Out** how it moves. Have the class guess what it is.

❸ **Share** your picture. Tell what else the living thing can do.

Build Background: Watch a video about how a plant grows.
⊙ **NGReach.com**

Describe

Listen and sing.

Song ((MP3))

I Love My Bike

I can eat and I can drink.
I am living.

I am healthy. I can think.
I am a living thing.

My bike can not eat.
My bike can not play.
It's nonliving.
That's OK.
I love it anyway!

Tune: "Camptown Races"

Key Words

People, plants, and animals are **living** .

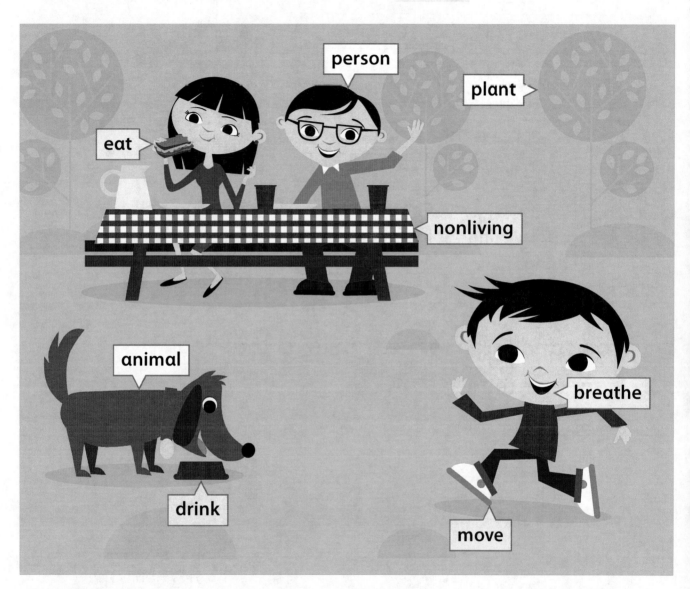

Talk Together

Talk Together

You are living. How do you know? Describe how something nonliving is different from something living.

List Facts

Living Things Checklist
can eat ☑
can drink ☑
is healthy ☑
can think ☑

List facts about living things here.

Check off the facts here.

Look and listen for facts in texts that you hear and read.

It's nonliving!

Talk Together

Choose a **living** or **nonliving** thing in the classroom. Have a partner guess what it is using the checklist and other questions.

More Key Words

alive

plant

pot

A plant is **alive**.
A pot is not alive.

energy

Swimming takes a lot of **energy**.

exercise

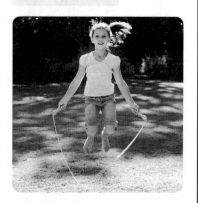

My heart beats fast when I **exercise**.

food

I like many kinds of **food**.

health

Brushing your teeth is good for your **health**.

Talk Together

Use one **Key Word** in a sentence.

I have a lot of energy today.

Add words to My Vocabulary Notebook.
NGReach.com

71

Read a Song

A **song** is words with music. You can sing a song.

✓ Look for **rhyme**. Listen to the **rhythm**.

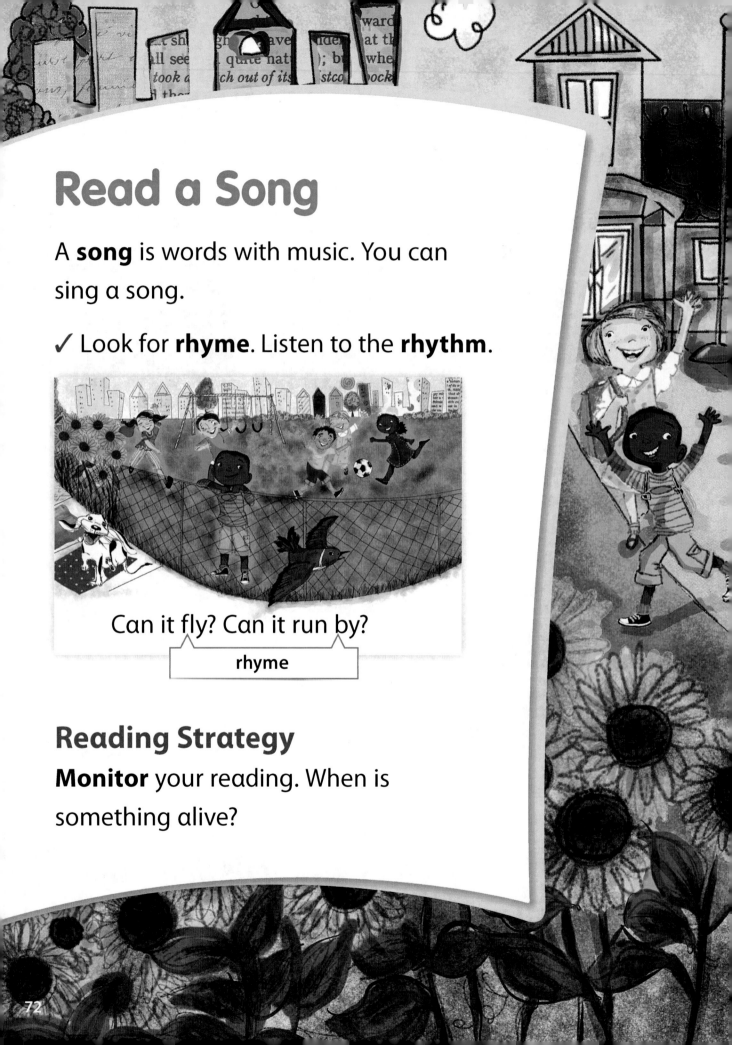

Can it fly? Can it run by?

rhyme

Reading Strategy

Monitor your reading. When is something alive?

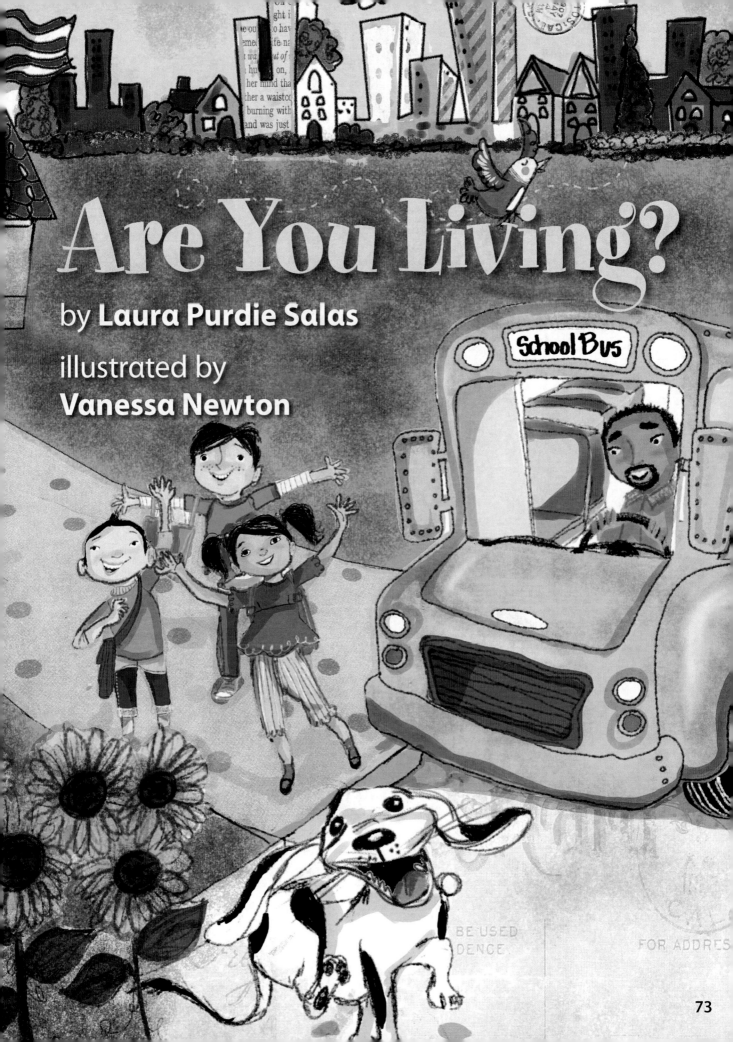

Are You Living?

by **Laura Purdie Salas**

illustrated by
Vanessa Newton

School Bus

Are you **living** ? Are you living?

Do you **eat**? Do you sleep?

If you need to **breathe** air,
Move from here to there, then

You're living. You're living.

Is it growing? Is it growing?

Toward the sky? Green and high?

If it needs damp ground and
Sunshine all around, then

It's a plant. It's a plant.

Is it moving? Is it moving?

Can it fly? Can it run by?

Living things need dinner,
Or they get much thinner.

So they need
To **drink** and feed. ❖

Talk About It

1. What happens to a **living** thing if it does not **eat**?

   If a living thing does not eat, it will ____ .

2. What helps a plant grow tall?

   ____ helps plants grow tall.

3. How do you know if something is **nonliving**?

   Something is nonliving if ____ .

Learn test-taking strategies.
NGReach.com

Write About It

Living things **move** in different ways.
How do you like to move?

I like to ____ and ____ .

List Facts

What other facts did you learn about living things? Add to the checklist.

Living Things Checklist	
can eat	☑
can drink	☑
is healthy	☑
can think	☑
	☐
	☐
	☐

With a partner, look through the pictures in the song. What is living and nonliving in each picture? Use your checklist.

The flower grows.

I grow, too.

Sort Words

Living Things	Nonliving Things
boy	ball
dog	flag
plant	clock

You can sort these words in a group because they are alike. They are all **Living Things**.

You can sort these words in a group because they are alike. They are all **Nonliving Things**.

Try It Together

Use picture cards. Sort the words into two groups. Talk about how the words in each group are alike and different.

Connect Across Texts You read about what makes something **living**. Now read about how one living thing becomes **nonliving**.

Genre A **diagram** uses steps to show how something is made.

A Straw Hat

by **Lily Block**

1 These living plants grow tall and green.

2 A farmer cuts down the plants. The farmer collects the plants.

Straw begins as a **living** thing.

3 The dry plants are straw.

4 The straw is made into a hat. The hat is nonliving.

A straw hat is a **nonliving** thing.

Compare Genres

How are "Are You Living?" and "A Straw Hat" different?

Song

Toward the sky? Green and high?

rhyming words

79

Diagram

❶ These living plants grow tall and green.

❷ A farmer cuts down the plants. The farmer collects the plants.

Straw begins as a **living** thing.

90

numbered steps

Talk Together

Think about what you read. When is something **alive**?

Grammar

Skills Trace: ▶ Adjectives: Color, Size, and Shape
▶ Adjectives: How Many/How Much
▶ **Adjectives:** Color, Size, and Shape

Adjectives

An **adjective** describes, or tells about, a **noun**.

A red machine collects the tall plants.

Grammar Rules Adjectives

Adjectives tell how something looks. They tell about:
- **Size**
- **Color**
- **Shape**

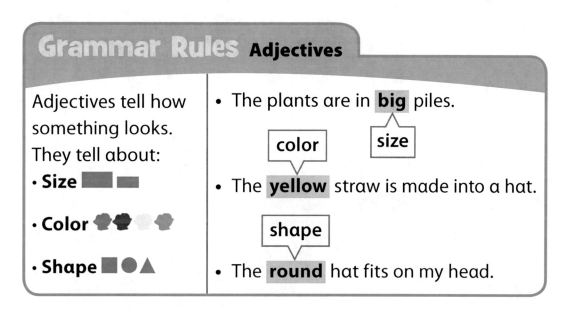

- The plants are in **big** piles. color size
- The **yellow** straw is made into a hat. shape
- The **round** hat fits on my head.

Read a Sentence

Which words below are adjectives? How do you know?

The red ribbon is on the small hat.

Write a Sentence

Think about a shirt you have. Write a sentence to tell about it. Use an adjective. Read the sentence to a partner.

Retell a Story

Listen and sing.   **Song** ((MP3))

Ant and the Grasshopper

I will retell a story
About a smart ant
And a lazy grasshopper
That did not like to plan.

In the hot summer,
Ant looked for seeds.
When winter days came,
Ant had good food to eat.

Grasshopper did not work.
All summer he played.
But then he was hungry
On cold winter days.

Tune: "On Top of Old Smokey"

Key Words

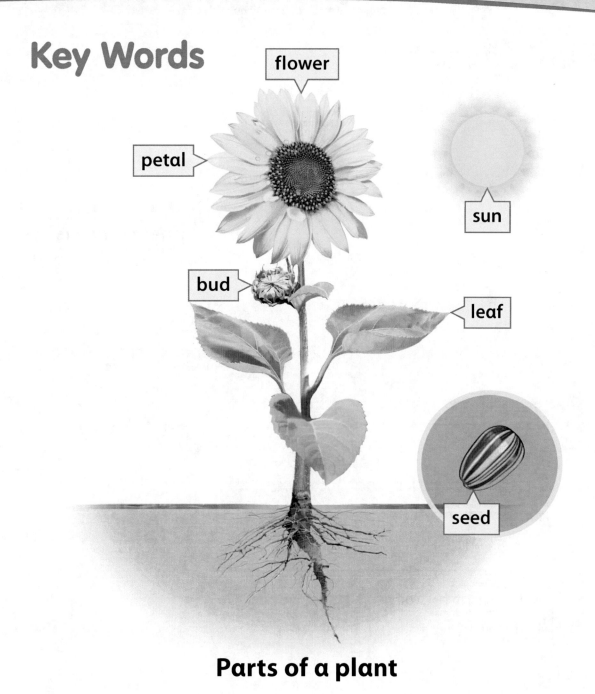

flower

petal

sun

bud

leaf

seed

Parts of a plant

Look at this living plant. Talk about its parts. Use the diagram to make up a story. Retell the story to a friend.

Identify Plot

Character-Setting-Plot Chart

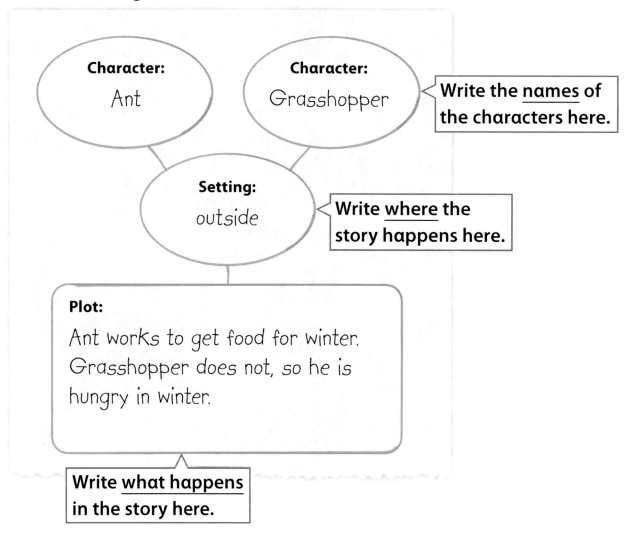

Character:
Ant

Character:
Grasshopper

Write the **names** of the characters here.

Setting:
outside

Write **where** the story happens here.

Plot:

Ant works to get food for winter. Grasshopper does not, so he is hungry in winter.

Write **what happens** in the story here.

Talk Together

Retell a story you know to a partner. Write the title. Then fill out a character-setting-plot chart. Take turns.

Academic Vocabulary

height

This basketball player's **height** is seven feet.

length

The **length** of the carrot is 7 inches.

light

The **light** is bright.

project

I am so proud of my science fair **project**.

ready

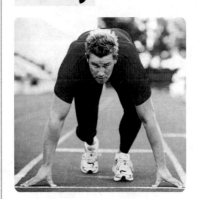

The runner is **ready** to race.

Talk Together

Ask a question using a **Key Word**.

What is the height of that tree?

Add words to My Vocabulary Notebook.
NGReach.com

Read a Folk Tale

What happens in the folk tale?

A folk tale has a **plot**. A plot is what happens in a story.

A seed sleeps.

The seed becomes a flower.

Reading Strategy

Monitor your reading. What happens to the seed?

The Daisy

by **Lada Josefa Kratky**

illustrated by **Vicki Wehrman**

A little **seed** sleeps under the earth.

The **sun** shines. The rain falls.

One morning, the sun rises.

The sun knocks on the door.

The sun asks the little seed to come out and play.

The little seed says she just wants
to sleep.

A raindrop knocks on the door.

The raindrop asks the little seed to
come out and play.

The little seed says she just wants
to sleep.

The little seed goes back to sleep.

Time passes. The sun rises.
More rain falls.

The sun and the rain knock on the
little seed's door.

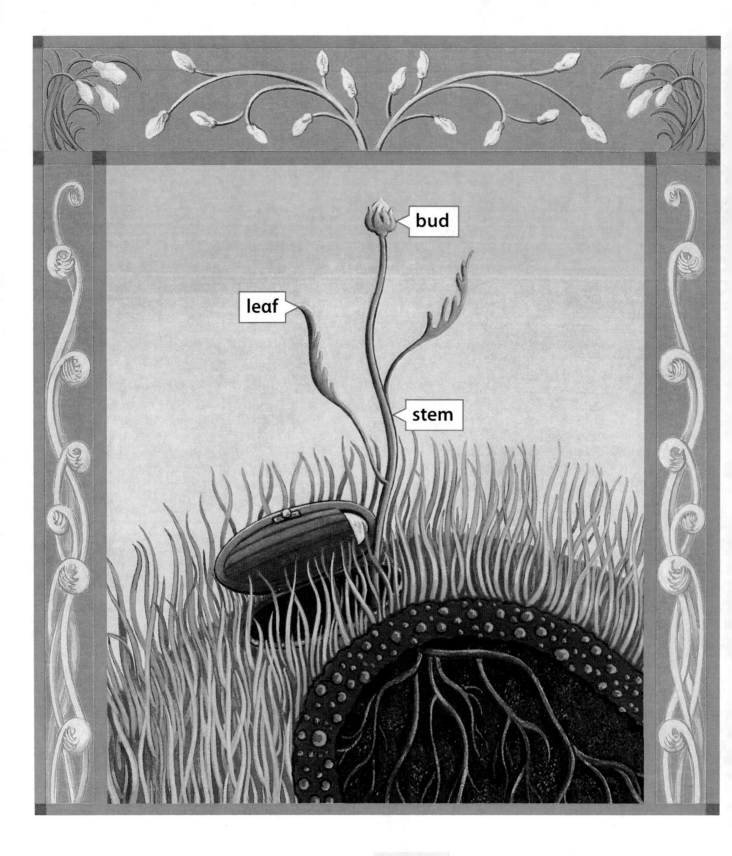

The door opens. A **leaf** grows. Then a little **bud** grows.

One **petal** opens. Then many more open!

The little daisy smiles.

The daisy says hello to her friends.
She is **ready** to play now.

The sun, the rain, and
the daisy play together. ❖

Meet the Author

Lada Josefa Kratky

Lada Josefa Kratky grew up in Uruguay. Today she lives in California.

Lada writes books in both English and Spanish. She has written many wonderful folk tales!

▲ Lada Josefa Kratky

Writer's Craft

Find details that Lada Josefa Kratky uses to describe how a seed grows into a flower. How do the details help you understand what happens?

Talk About It

1. **What does the little seed grow up to be?**

    The little seed grows up to be a ____ .

2. **Why do the sun and the raindrop knock at the little seed's door?**

    They want the little seed to ____ .

3. **How do the sun and the raindrop help the little seed?**

    They give her ____ .

Write About It

What does a seed need in order to grow?
Write one sentence. Read it aloud.

A seed needs the sun to grow.

Identify Plot

Complete the chart for *The Daisy.*

Character-Setting-Plot Chart

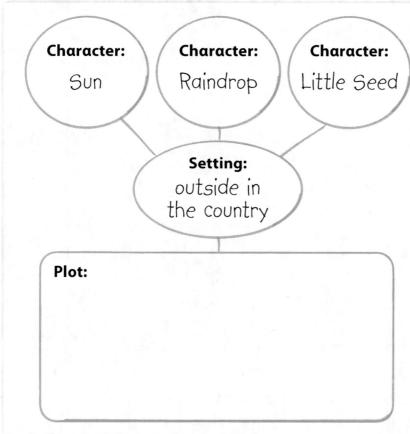

Use your character-setting-plot chart to describe what happens to the little seed.

The little seed will not play with the sun because she only wants to sleep.

119

Sort Words

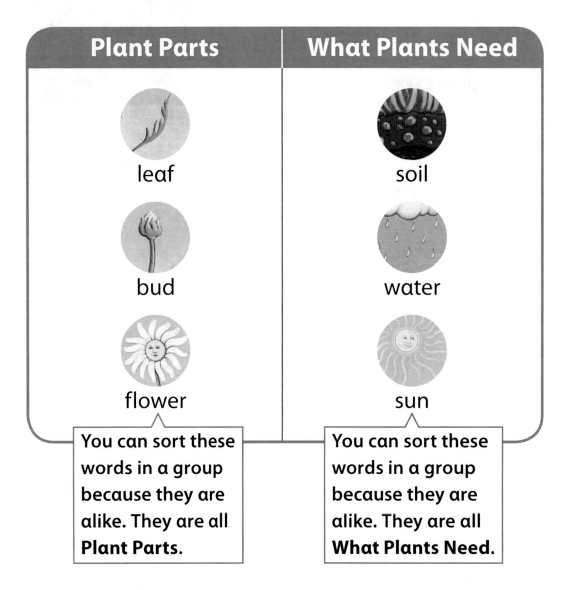

Plant Parts	What Plants Need
leaf	soil
bud	water
flower	sun

You can sort these words in a group because they are alike. They are all **Plant Parts**.

You can sort these words in a group because they are alike. They are all **What Plants Need**.

Try It Together

Write the words on cards. Sort the cards into two groups: **Kinds of Plants** and **Where Plants Grow**. Talk about why each word belongs in its group.

daisy
garden
flowerpot
sunflower

Connect Across Texts You read about how a **seed** becomes a **flower** and is alive. Now read about giant redwood trees.

Genre A **project notebook** shows what someone is studying. It uses words and photos.

Michael Fay and the Giant Redwoods

by **Gabrielle Burns**

Michael Fay studies redwood trees.
They are one of the biggest living
things on Earth!

Redwood trees can grow to a **height** of 360 feet!

Redwood Coast

CALIFORNIA

Redwoods grow in California. California has what redwoods need to grow.

fog

Redwoods need warm, wet weather. They get a lot of water from fog.

Compare Genres

How are the words in *The Daisy* and "Michael Fay and the Giant Redwoods" different?

Folk Tale

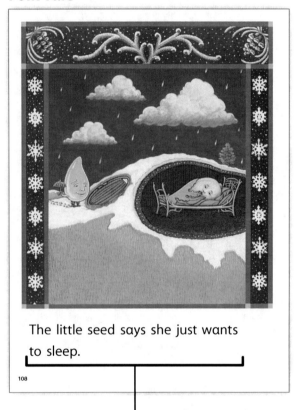

The little seed says she just wants to sleep.

108

A folk tale is a fantasy.
A seed can talk.

Project Notebook

Redwood trees can grow to a **height** of 360 feet!

123

A project notebook is nonfiction. It has facts.

Talk Together

Think about what you read. When is something alive?

Adjectives

An **adjective** describes, or tells about, a **noun**.

One child sees many trees in the forest.

Grammar Rules Adjectives

Adjectives tell **how many** or **how much**.	• Michael walks **two** miles. how many • He stands next to **several** trees. how much

Read a Sentence

Which word below is an adjective? How do you know?

Michael photographs five trees.

Write a Sentence

Write a sentence that describes the redwoods. Use an adjective that tells "how many" or "how much".

Write Like a Teacher

Write How to Make Something

You can make a hat with straw. What else can you make with plants? Explain how to make something with plants. Write for your classmates.

How to Make a Seed Picture

by Pham Thi Mai

What You Need

list ▷ pencil   paper

         glue   seeds

What You Do

directions ▷ 1. Draw a picture on the paper.

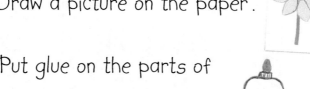

2. Put glue on the parts of the picture where you want seeds.

3. Press the seeds onto the glue Let it dry.

❶ Plan and Write

Talk with a partner about plants and plant parts. Draw pictures of what you can make with plants. Pick one thing and describe it to your partner.

Write what you will need. Then write what to do. List the steps in order.

❷ Check Your Work

Revise and edit your writing. Use this checklist.

❸ Finish and Share

Finish your writing. Leave space between steps. Number the steps. Draw a picture to show each step.

Read your writing aloud. Speak clearly. Share what you know.

Checklist

☑ Think about the group, What You Need. Did you remember to write all the things that belong in this group?

☑ Did you use adjectives to describe how things look or feel?

☑ Read each word of your work. Say aloud the syllables. Circle words to check. Correct spelling errors.

I need sunflower seeds.

When is something alive?

Share Your Ideas

Think about what living things do and what they need. When is something alive? Choose one of these ways to share your ideas about the **Big Question**.

Write It!

Make a Chart
Draw a T chart. Write these headings: Living Things and Nonliving Things. Draw and label pictures to go under each heading.

Talk About It!

Tell a Tale

Make up a new folk tale about a plant and a rock. The group decides on character names and a setting. Then, each person in the group tells part of the plot. Take turns.

> A small plant and a big rock lived in the forest.

Do It! ✋

Make a Puppet

Use a sock to make a puppet of Zina. Then make Zina come alive! Show what she can say and do. Use your sock puppets to have a puppet show.

To Your Front Door

? BIG Question

How do we get what we need?

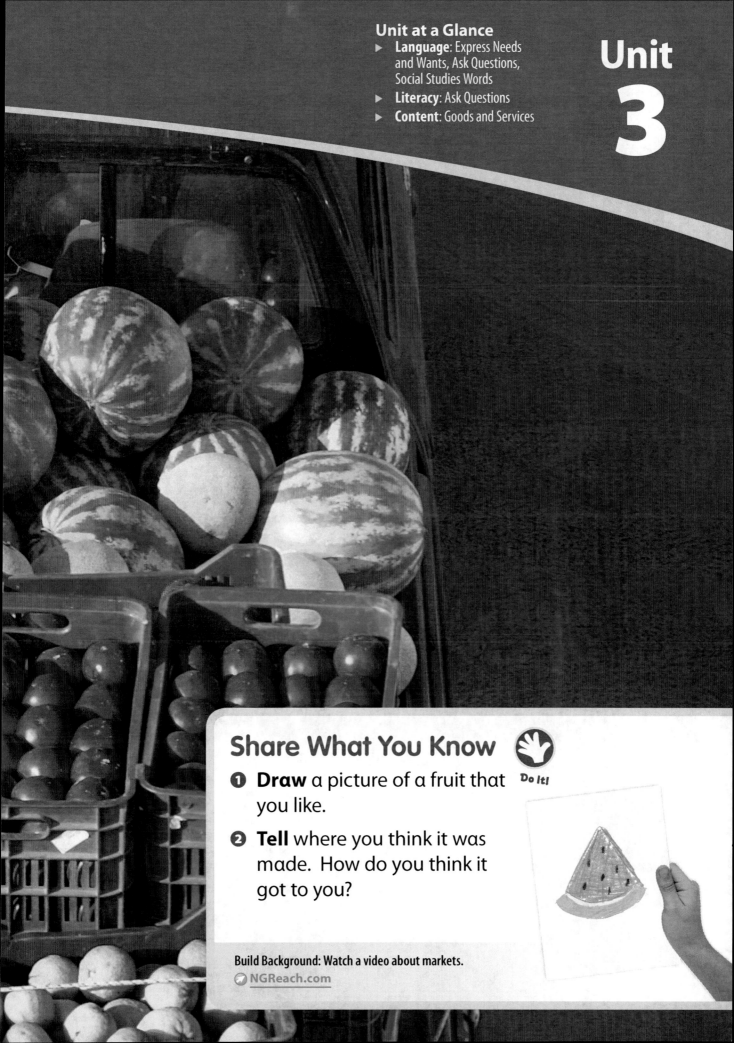

Unit at a Glance
▶ **Language**: Express Needs and Wants, Ask Questions, Social Studies Words
▶ **Literacy**: Ask Questions
▶ **Content**: Goods and Services

Unit 3

Share What You Know

❶ **Draw** a picture of a fruit that you like.

Do It!

❷ **Tell** where you think it was made. How do you think it got to you?

Build Background: Watch a video about markets.
NGReach.com

Express Needs and Wants

Listen and sing.   *Song* (((MP3)))

To Market

I **need** peas.

I need fish.

These two **things**

Are on my list.

At the market

They sell toys

Both big and small.

I **want** a car.

I want a ball.

Tune: "This Old Man"

Key Words

At the **market**

▲ They **shop** at the market. They **buy** food.

Talk Together

Look at the market. What do you need to buy at the market? What do you want to buy?

Categorize

T Chart

Need	Want
• peas	• toy car
• fish	• ball
•	•
•	•

On one side of the chart, list what you need.

On the other side, list what you want.

Talk Together

Choose eight picture cards. With a partner, sort them into Wants and Needs piles. Then add the items to the chart.

136

More Key Words

business

My father owns a flower **business**.

• goods

Stores sell these **goods**.

job

My mom has a **job** at a bank.

• needs

Food and clothing are **needs**.

• wants

Toys and games are **wants**.

Talk Together

Give clues for a **Key Word** for a partner to guess.

> This word can be a store. It starts with a b.

• High Frequency Word

Add words to My Vocabulary Notebook.
NGReach.com

Read a Social Studies Article

A **social studies article** is nonfiction.
It tells about real things.

✓ Look for headings.

What Markets Sell `heading`

Markets sell fish.

Reading Strategy

Ask questions as you read. What kinds of markets are there?

Markets

by Cassie Mayer

Markets Around the World

People **shop** at **markets**.

Markets **sell** many things.

spices

People sell things at markets.

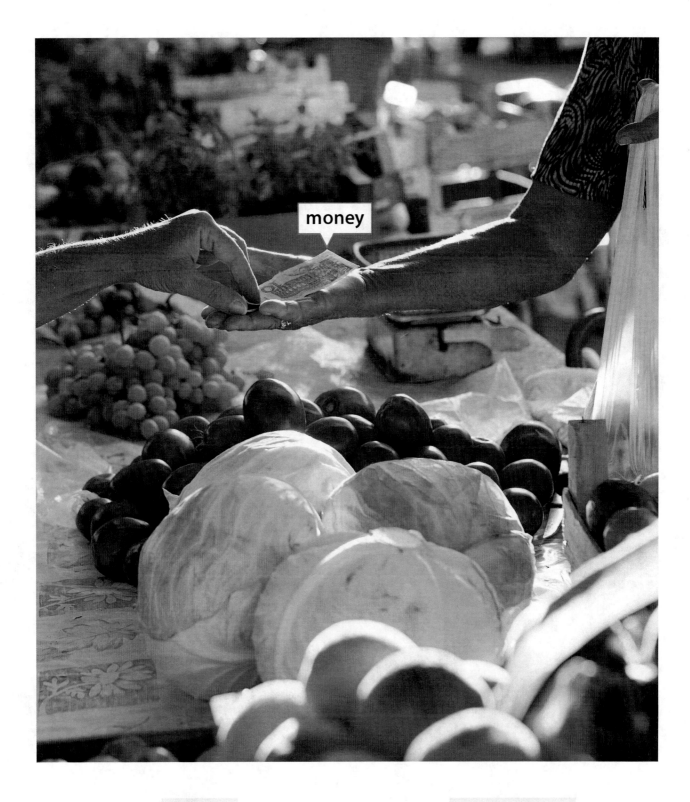

People **buy** things with **money**.

Types of Markets

Markets are big.

Markets are small.

Markets are on streets.

Markets are in malls.

Markets sell fish.

Markets sell cheese.

Markets sell clothes.

Markets sell toys.

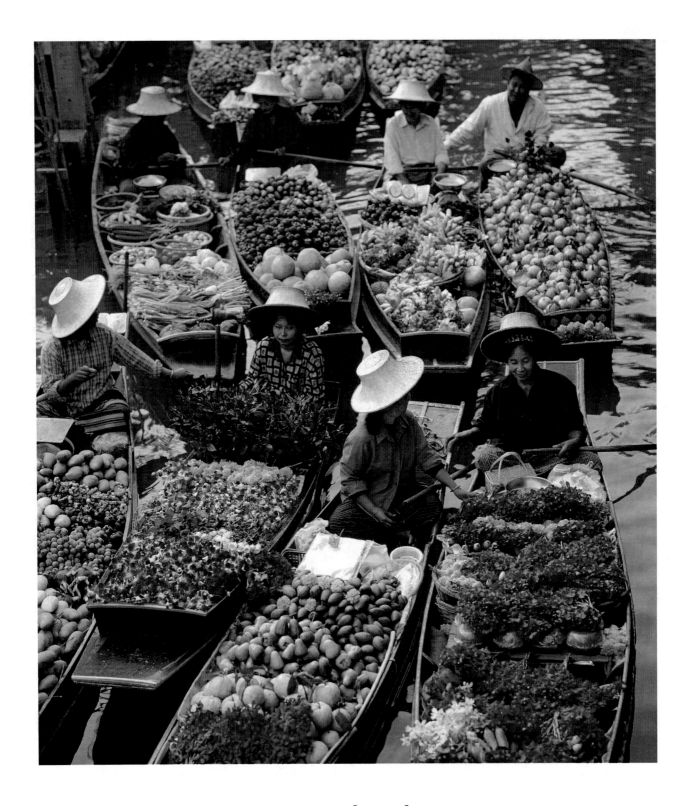

Markets are special wherever
you go.

People **need** markets. ❖

Talk About It

1. Name three things that **markets** **sell**.

   Markets sell ____ , ____ , and ____ .

2. How are markets different?

   Some markets ____ . Some markets ____ .

3. Why do people **need** markets?

   People need markets to ____ .

Learn test-taking strategies.
NGReach.com

Write About It

Write two questions you had as you read about markets.

What is ____ ?
Where ____ ?

Categorize

Markets are alike and different. What do they sell?

T Chart

Type of Market	What it Sells
• fruit market	• bananas, pears, grapes
•	•
•	•

Use your chart. Tell a partner what you learned in *Markets*.

> Markets sell fish and cheese.

Identify Verbs

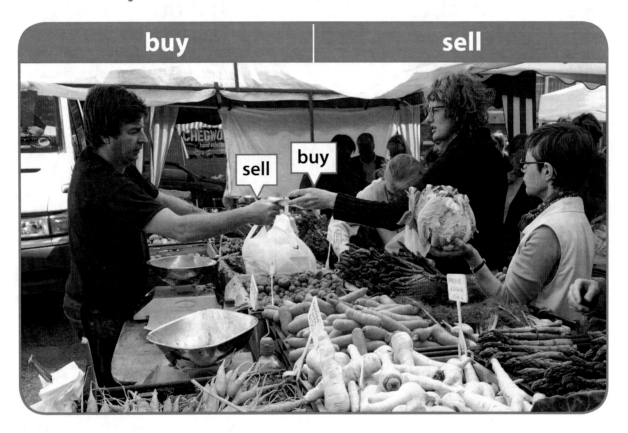

| buy | sell |

Buy and **sell** are **action verbs**. An action verb tells what someone or something does.

> She **buys** lettuce.
> He **sells** vegetables.

Try It Together

Talk about these words. Act out the words that are action verbs.

desk	man
shop	clap
jump	orange

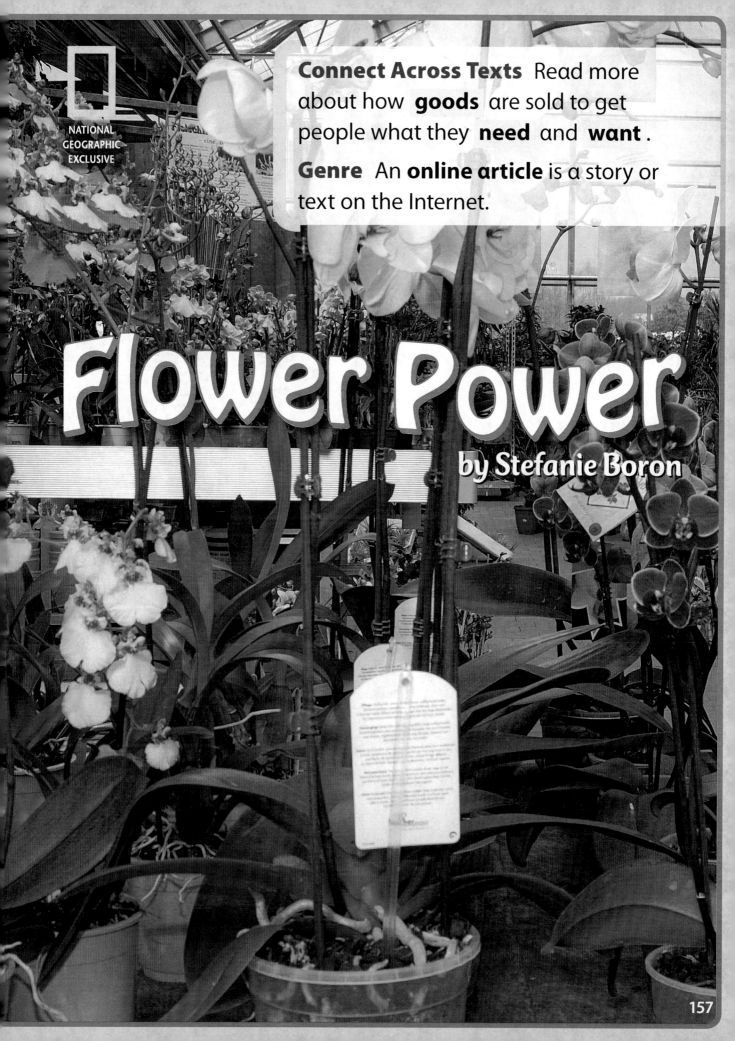

Connect Across Texts Read more about how **goods** are sold to get people what they **need** and **want**.

Genre An **online article** is a story or text on the Internet.

Flower Power

by Stefanie Boron

Home 🏠   Stories 📖   Photos 📷   Videos 🎬   🔍 Search ▸

Farmers Sell Flowers to Save Land

by **Stefanie Boron**

September 21, 2009– Farmers in Brazil grow crops. Cid Simoes and Paola Segura had an idea to help farmers save land.

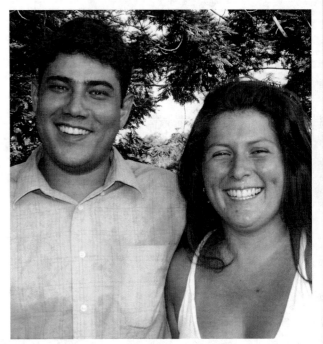

▲ **Cid Simoes and Paola Segura**

▲ **These are soybean crops. They need a lot of land to grow.**

NEXT »

The forests of Brazil have beautiful plants and flowers. People around the world want to **buy** them.

Farmers can **sell** these plants and flowers instead of crops.

▲ Brazilian orchid

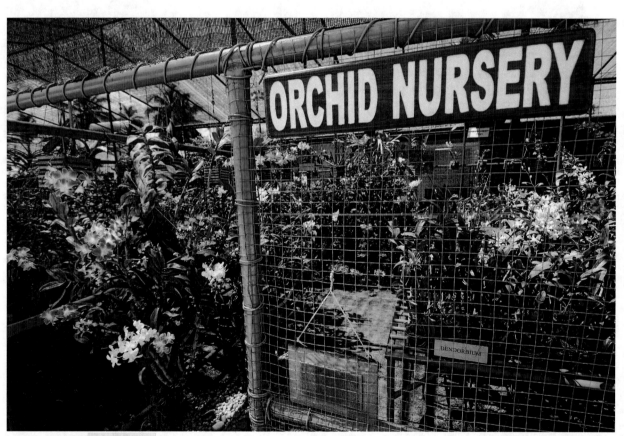

▲ Orchid **market**

≪ PREVIOUS

Compare Author's Purpose

Articles have different topics. Authors write articles for different reasons.

Markets

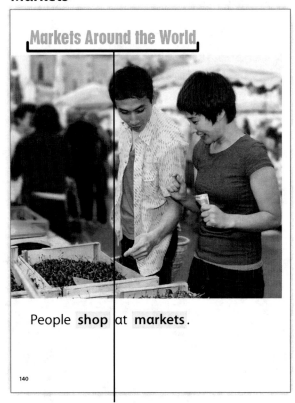

The topic of this article is markets around the world.

Flower Power

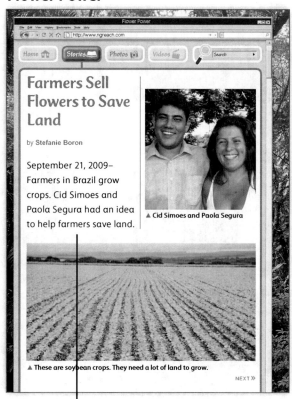

The author's purpose for writing this article is to tell about flower farmers in Brazil.

Talk Together

Think about what you read and learned. How do we get what we need and **want**?

Present Tense Verbs

Some **verbs** tell about actions that happen **in the present**. The actions happen **now**.

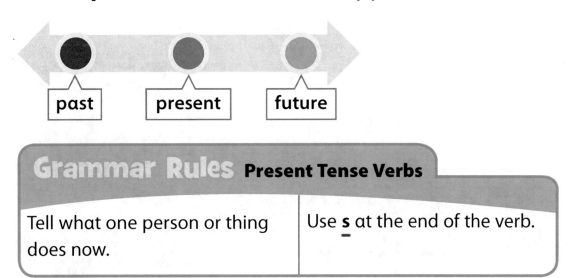

Tell what one person or thing does now.	Use **s** at the end of the verb.

Grammar Rules Present Tense Verbs

Read a Sentence

Why does the verb below have **s**?

The girl **buys** flowers.

Write a Sentence

Write a sentence about a farmer in Brazil. Write about what a farmer does now. Read it to a partner.

High Frequency
Words

how

what

where

Ask Questions

Listen and sing.   *Song*

Shopping

I want to buy this set of markers.

Where can I buy all of them?

What other things can I get there?

I also need red and blue pens.

Let's go, let's go.

Let's go today to the

office store.

Let's go, let's go.

How do we get to the store?

Tune: "My Bonnie Lies Over the Ocean"

Key Words

Shoes to You: A How-to

1. Make it in a **factory**.

2. Send, or **ship**, it on a truck.

3. The **delivery** comes to the **store**. Buy it!

4. Bring it home to your **neighborhood**.

Talk Together

Use the picture. Follow the steps in order. Ask a partner questions about how shoes get to your neighborhood.

Identify Details

Idea Web

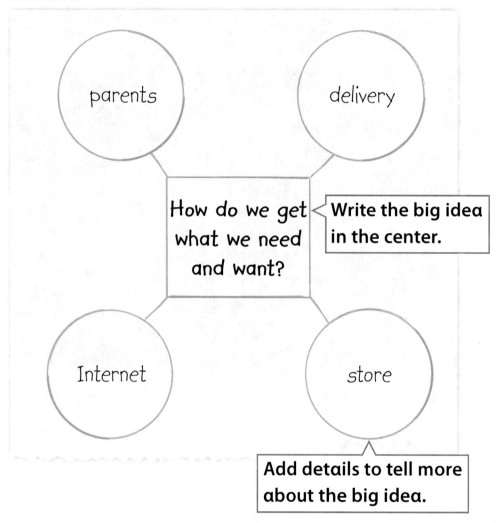

parents

delivery

How do we get what we need and want?

Write the big idea in the center.

Internet

store

Add details to tell more about the big idea.

Talk Together

Make an idea web. Write "What do I need for school?" in the center. Fill in the details. Share it with a partner. How are your details the same?

More Key Words

bring

I **bring** my backpack to school.

count

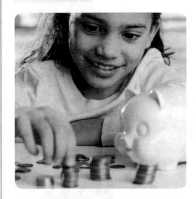

I **count** my money to see what I can buy.

earn

The boy works to **earn** money.

service

A **service** is work someone does for money, such as cutting hair.

worker

A **worker** at the restaurant makes breakfast.

Talk Together

Draw a picture of a **Key Word** for your partner to label.

worker

Add words to My Vocabulary Notebook.
🔵 NGReach.com

Read a Poem

✓ Look for rhyming words.

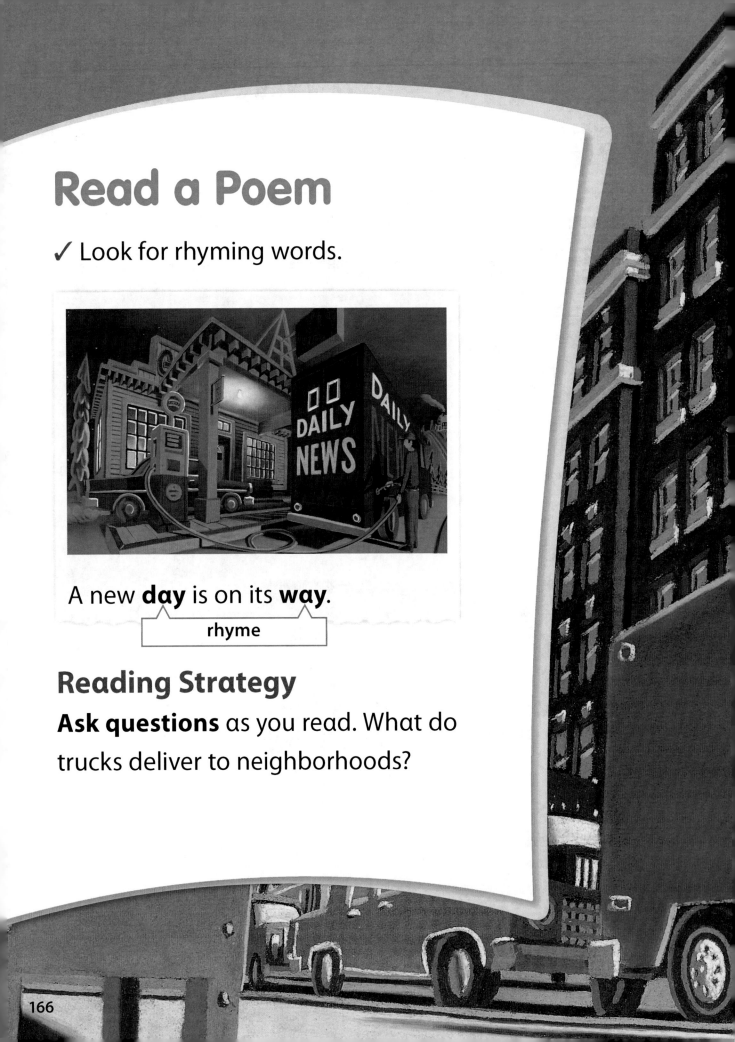

A new **day** is on its **way**.

rhyme

Reading Strategy

Ask questions as you read. What do trucks deliver to neighborhoods?

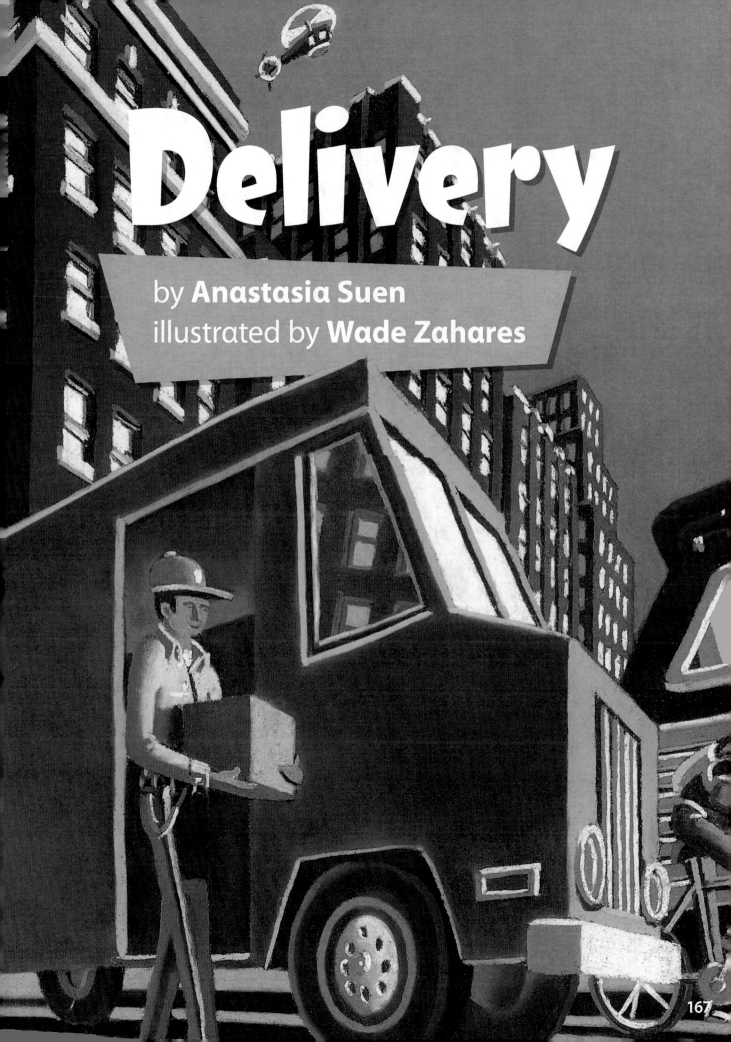

Delivery

by **Anastasia Suen**
illustrated by **Wade Zahares**

A new day is on its way.

Papers come one by one.

Boxes and cans come
in trucks and vans.

Unwrap it all for shelves on the wall.

wing

Wheels and wings carry
many things.

wheels

High and low, we come and go.

Trucks on roads carry loads.

loads

Trains speed by. Hello! Goodbye!

Containers wait at number eight.

A new day is on its way.

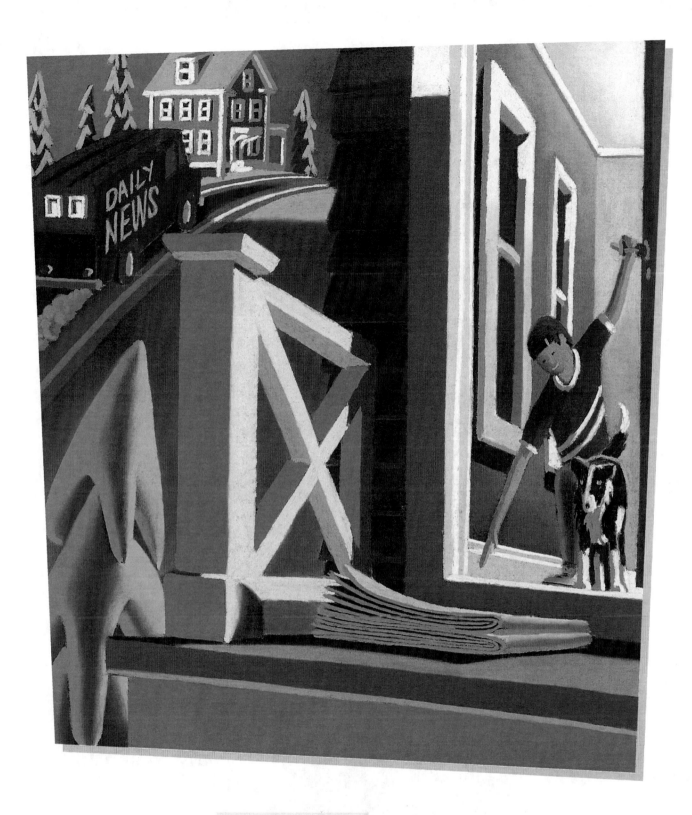

Delivery! ❖

Meet the Author

Anastasia Suen

Anastasia Suen has written more than 100 books! She likes to write about real things.

Ms. Suen used to be a first grade teacher. Today she visits schools as an author.

▲ Anastasia Suen

Writer's Craft

Anastasia Suen uses verbs, such as **carry**, **speed**, and **wait**, in her poem. What are three other verbs you can use to describe deliveries?

Meet the Illustrator
Wade Zahares

Wade Zahares sells paintings and uses others in children's books.

Mr. Zahares had to practice to become a good artist. Now, he loves to paint whenever he can.

▲ Wade Zahares

Talk About It

1. How are boxes and cans **delivered**?

Boxes and cans are delivered ____ .

2. What would happen if there were no deliveries?

If there were no deliveries, ____ .

3. Which words in the poem rhyme?

____ and ____ rhyme.

Learn test-taking strategies.
NGReach.com

Write About It

Read this sentence. Which words rhyme?

Trucks on roads carry loads.

Write a new rhyme poem about a delivery.

____ deliver ____ .

Identify Details

How do goods get to **stores** in *Delivery*?

Idea Web

Use your web. Tell a partner what happens in *Delivery*.

A truck delivers goods to stores.

Identify Verbs

carry	ship

Carry and **ship** are **action verbs**. An action verb tells what someone or something does.

> The workers **carry** boxes.
> We **ship** goods on planes.

Try It Together

Read these sentences with a partner. Find the action verbs.

> I find a shirt at the store.
> I ask my dad for the shirt.
> I wear the new shirt home.

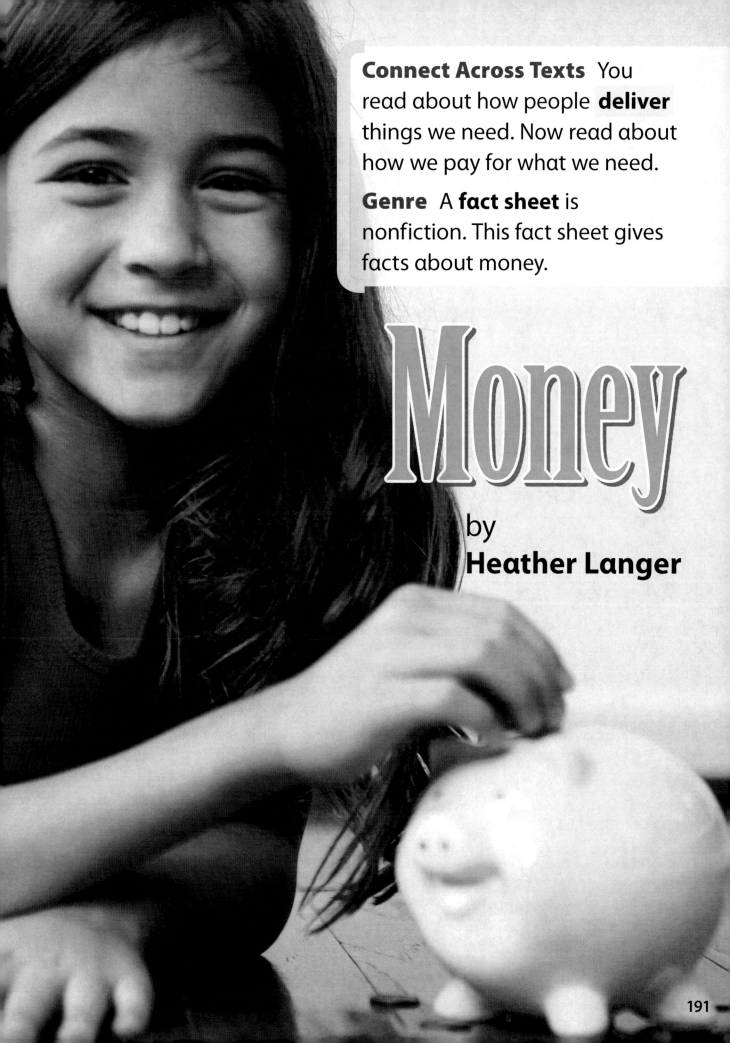

Connect Across Texts You read about how people **deliver** things we need. Now read about how we pay for what we need.

Genre A **fact sheet** is nonfiction. This fact sheet gives facts about money.

Money

by
Heather Langer

Money can be paper.

one dollar bill

five dollar bill

ten dollar bill

twenty dollar bill

Money can be coins.

penny = one cent
1¢

nickel = five cents
5¢

dime = ten cents
10¢

quarter = twenty-five cents
25¢

People pay money for things they need.

People save money for things they want.

Compare Genres

How are *Delivery* and "Money" different?

Poem

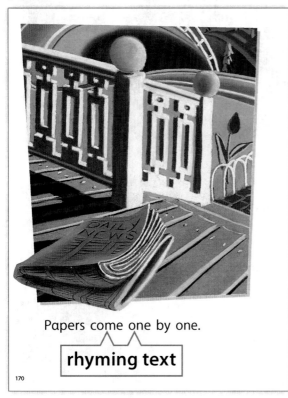

Papers come one by one.

rhyming text

170

Fact Sheet

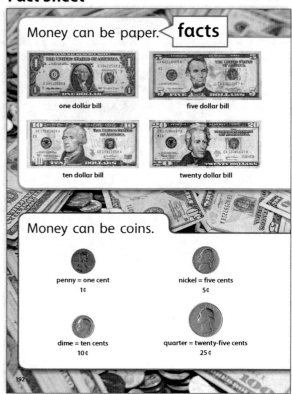

Money can be paper. facts

one dollar bill   five dollar bill

ten dollar bill   twenty dollar bill

Money can be coins.

penny = one cent   nickel = five cents
1¢   5¢

dime = ten cents   quarter = twenty-five cents
10¢   25¢

192

Talk Together

Think about what you read and learned. How do we get what we need and want?

Grammar and Spelling

Skills Trace: ▶ Verb *to be*
▶ Verb *to have*
⊙ **Verbs *be* and *have***

Subject-Verb Agreement: be and *have*

Some **verbs** do not show action, such as **be** and **have**.

The truck **is** big. The truck **has** a flat tire. ⟨ **tells about one thing**

The boxes **are** heavy. The boxes **have** cans in them. ⟨ **tells about more than one thing**

Grammar Rules **Subject-Verb Agreement**

be in present tense

To tell about one person, place, or thing, use **is**.
To tell about more than one, use **are**.

have in present tense

To tell about one person, place, or thing, use **has**.
To tell about more than one, use **have**.

Read a Sentence

Why is the verb *have* used in the sentence?

Three trucks **have** big wheels.

Write a Sentence

Write a sentence about one van. Use the verb *be*.

195

Write as a Family Member

Write a Thank You Letter

Think about a gift. Tell why the gift is special. Write a thank you letter for the gift.

May 1

Dear Aunt Olga,

Thank you for the gift. I like it a lot. I needed a backpack for my books. I wanted a pink one. Where did you get it? I didn't see this style when I went to the store!

Love,
Sophie

Write the date and the person's name in the greeting.

Sophie tells why she **needed** and **wanted** the gift.

Write a closing and sign your name.

❶ Plan and Write

Work with a partner. Make a list of special gifts from family members. Pick one gift.

Write sentences to say thank you. Then write sentences that tell why you needed and wanted the gift.

❷ Check Your Work

Revise and edit your writing. Use this checklist.

❸ Finish and Share

Finish your thank you letter. Make sure you used the right greeting and closing.

Read the thank you letter to a friend. Speak clearly. Then give the letter to your family member who gave you the gift. Say *thank you* again!

Checklist

☑ Think about different verbs you can use. Can you use verbs that show action?

☑ Check your sentences. Do your subjects and verbs go together?

☑ Read your own work. Trace words with your finger. Check for backwords letters. Correct spelling errors.

> I really like this gift! Thanks!

197

Share Your Ideas

Think about the things we use every day. How do we get what we need? Choose one of these ways to share your ideas about the **Big Question**.

Write It!

Make a T Chart

Make a T Chart with a partner. Write these headings: Things We Buy and Things That Are Free. Write three things for each side of the chart.

Things We Buy	Things That Are Free
shoes	friends
milk	sunshine
toys	the park

Talk About It!

Rhyming Fun

Read this poem. Have each person in the group add to it. Say a want or a need that rhymes with one of the words. Then make new rhymes.

> I want a hug.
> I want a bug.
> I need some food.
> I need two shoes.

Do It!

Sort Wants and Needs

Cut pictures out of magazines of things you want and need. Make two folders. Label them. Put the pictures in the correct folder.

Want

Growing and Changing

How do animals change as they grow?

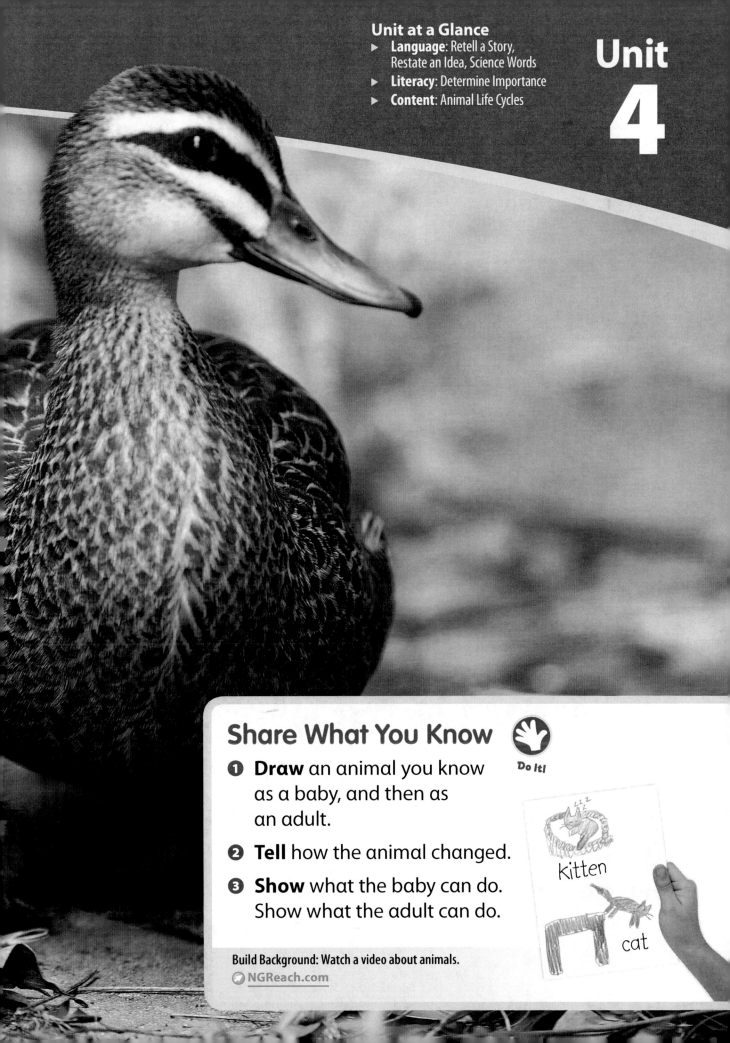

Unit at a Glance
▶ **Language**: Retell a Story, Restate an Idea, Science Words
▶ **Literacy**: Determine Importance
▶ **Content**: Animal Life Cycles

Unit
4

Share What You Know

Do It!

❶ **Draw** an animal you know as a baby, and then as an adult.

❷ **Tell** how the animal changed.

❸ **Show** what the baby can do. Show what the adult can do.

Build Background: Watch a video about animals.
🌐 NGReach.com

kitten

cat

Retell a Story

Listen and chant.

The Little Duckling

Chant ((MP3))

First, the little duckling
Hatches in a nest.
Mother Duck says
He's not like the rest.

Next, the bigger ducklings
Don't want to play.
The little duckling cries.
Then, he runs away.

Finally, he's happy,
Swimming in the pond.
For now the little duckling
Has grown into a swan.

Key Words

How do animals grow and change?

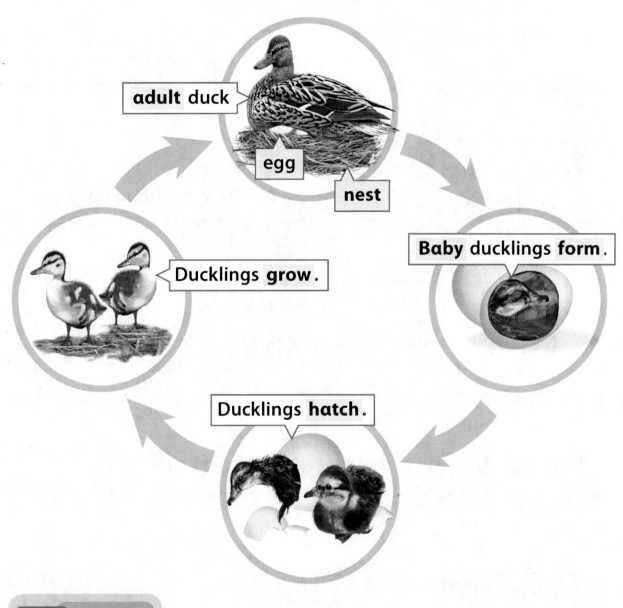

adult duck

egg

nest

Baby ducklings **form**.

Ducklings **grow**.

Ducklings **hatch**.

Talk Together

Look at the baby ducklings. How do they change as they grow? Use sequence words like first, next, and then.

Identify Plot

Begining-Middle-End Chart

Beginning:

The little duckling hatches.
He doesn't look like the rest.

> What happens first in the story? Write it here.

Middle:

No one likes the little duckling.
He runs away.

> What happens next? Write it here.

End:

The little duckling turns into a swan.

> What happens last? Write it here.

Look for the plot as you listen and read.

Talk Together

Think of a story you know. Use a beginning-middle-end chart to write or draw the plot. Then use the chart to retell your story.

More Key Words

before

One comes **before** two.

inside

The books are **inside** the box.

shape

The **shape** of a ball is round.

size

My dad's shoes are not my **size**.

• time

Seven o'clock is the **time** we wake up.

Talk Together

Work with a partner to use each **Key Word** in a sentence.

It is time for recess.

• High Frequency Word

Add words to My Vocabulary Notebook.
NGReach.com

Read a Story

Who is in the story?

Ruby

Mother Duck
and Father Duck

Rufus, Rory, Rosie, and Rebecca

Reading Strategy

As you read, look at the text and pictures to **determine what is important** in the story.

Ruby in Her Own Time

by **Jonathan Emmett**

illustrated by **Rebecca Harry**

Once upon a **time** upon a **nest**,
there lived two ducks.

A mother duck and a father duck.

There were five **eggs** in the nest.
Mother Duck sat upon the nest
all day,
and all night,

in wind,
and in rain.

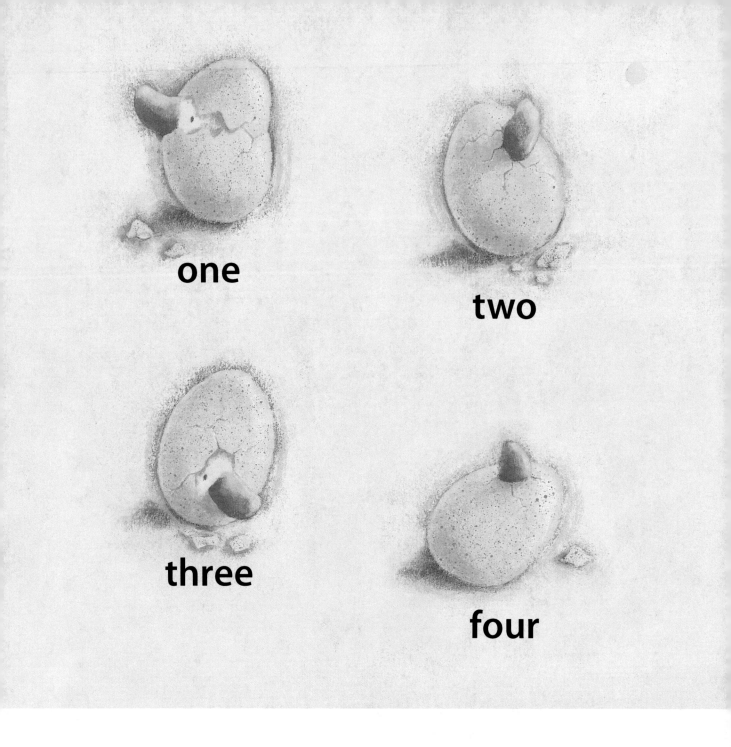

one

two

three

four

Then, one bright morning, the eggs began to **hatch**. Little beaks poked out into the sunlight.

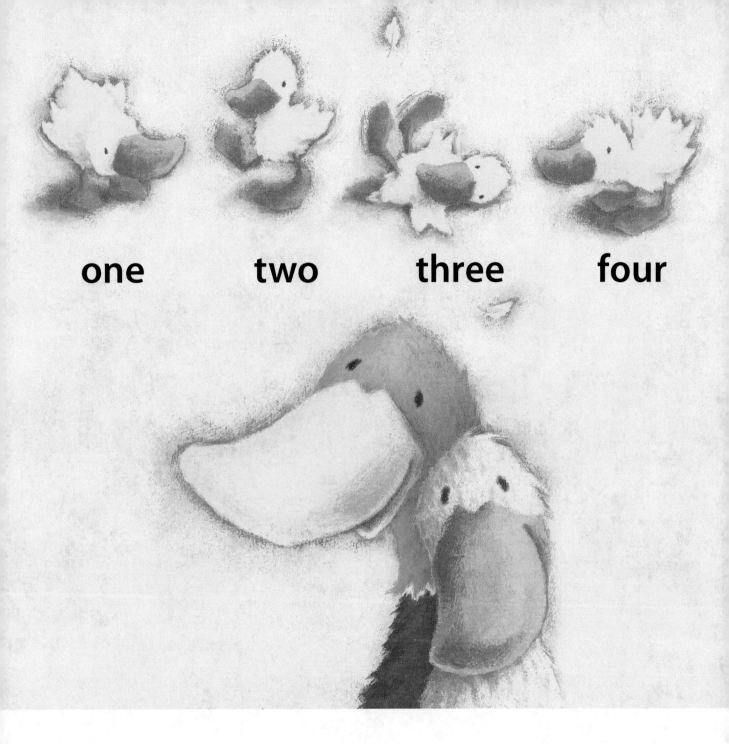

one   **two**   **three**   **four**

"We'll call them Rufus, Rory, Rosie, and Rebecca," said Father Duck.

But the fifth egg did nothing.
"Will it ever hatch?" asked
Father Duck.

"It will," said Mother Duck,
"in its own time."

And it did.

"We'll call her Ruby," said
Mother Duck, "because she's
small and precious."

Rufus, Rory, Rosie, and Rebecca
ate whatever they were given.
But Ruby ate nothing.

"Will she ever eat?" asked
Father Duck.
"She will," said Mother Duck,
"in her own time."

And she did.

Rufus, Rory, Rosie, and Rebecca

swam everywhere.

But Ruby swam nowhere.

"Will she ever swim?" asked
Father Duck.
"She will," said Mother Duck,
"in her own time."

And she did.

Rufus, Rory, Rosie, and
Rebecca grew bigger.

And Ruby grew bigger, too.
And when Rufus, Rory, Rosie, and
Rebecca began to fly . . .

Ruby flew, too.

Rufus, Rory, Rosie, and Rebecca
flew far and wide. They flew up
among the trees.

But Ruby flew farther and wider.

She flew up above the trees.

She stretched out her beautiful
wings. She flew high among
the clouds.

Mother Duck and Father Duck
watched Ruby fly away.

"Will she ever come back?" asked Mother Duck.

"She will," said Father Duck, "in her own time."

And she did. ❖

Meet the Author

Jonathan Emmett

Jonathan Emmett liked to read books and write stories when he was growing up.

Mr. Emmett gets lots of ideas from things that happen in real life. He keeps the ideas on his computer. That way, he won't forget to use them!

Writer's Craft

Find words that Jonathan Emmett repeats in the story. How does that make the story fun to read?

Talk About It

1. There are five **eggs**. Which egg is Ruby's?

The ____ egg is Ruby's.

2. What does it mean that Ruby does things in her own **time**?

It means ____ .

3. What happens after Ruby's wings **grow**?

After Ruby's wings grow, she ____ .

Learn test-taking strategies.
◯ NGReach.com

Write About It

Describe how Mother Duck and Father Duck feel about Ruby. How can you tell?

Mother Duck and Father Duck feel
____ . They ____ .

Identify Plot

What happens in this story? Use sequence words.

Begining-Middle-End Chart

Beginning:

First, Ruby hatches from an egg.

Middle:

End:

Use your chart to retell the story of *Ruby in Her Own Time*. Act out the events in order as you retell.

Ruby is the last egg to hatch.

Use Context Clues

word clues	meaning
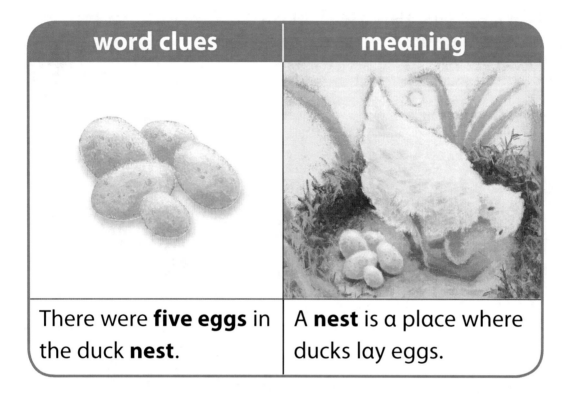	
There were **five eggs** in the duck **nest**.	A **nest** is a place where ducks lay eggs.

Look at the words and sentences around a new word. You might find **word clues** to figure out the meaning.

Try It Together

Read the sentences. What does the word **hatch** mean? Talk about the word clues.

Then one bright morning, the eggs began to **hatch**. Little beaks poked out into the sunlight.

Connect Across Texts You read about how Ruby changes. Now read about how turtles change as they **grow** .

Genre A **science article** is nonfiction. This article gives facts about turtles.

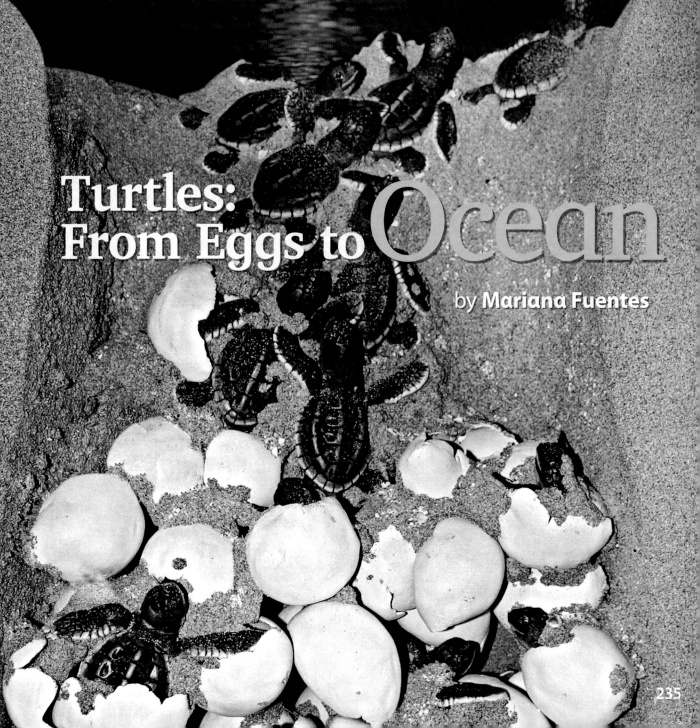

Turtles: From Eggs to Ocean

by **Mariana Fuentes**

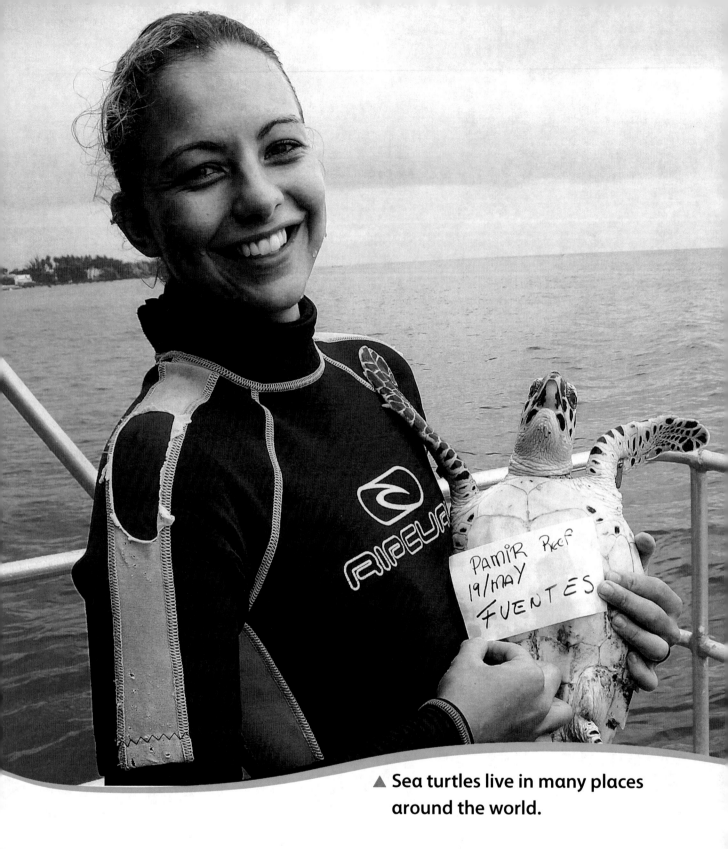

▲ Sea turtles live in many places around the world.

I am Mariana Fuentes. I study sea turtles.

▲ Turtles can lay
over 100 eggs!

Sea turtles live in water, but they
lay **eggs** on land.

▲ Turtles cover the eggs
with sand.

Turtles make **nests** for their eggs
in sand. They make a hole, and lay
eggs. The eggs will **hatch** in about
two months.

▲ When the turtles hatch, they run to the ocean.

All the turtles hatch at the same **time**. They will soon grow to be **adult** turtles. They can live to be 80 years old!

Compare Genres

How are *Ruby in Her Own Time* and "Turtles:
From Eggs to Ocean" different?

Animal Fantasy

"Will she ever eat?" asked
Father Duck.
"She will," said Mother Duck,
"in her own time."

219

animals talk

Science Article

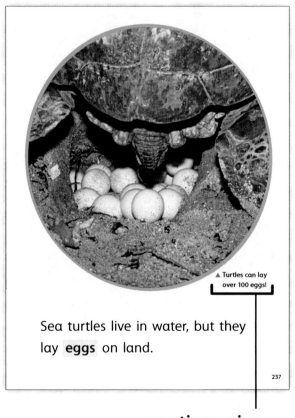

▲ Turtles can lay
over 100 eggs!

Sea turtles live in water, but they
lay **eggs** on land.

237

captions give
real information

Talk Together

Think about what you have read and learned.
How do animals change as they grow?

Grammar

Skills Trace: ▸ Singular Subject Pronouns: *I, you, it*
▸ Plural Subject Pronouns: *we, you, they*
▶ **Subject Pronoun Agreement**

Subject Pronouns

A **pronoun** can take the place of a **noun** .

Grammar Rules Subject Pronouns

Use **I** for yourself. Always use a capital letter for **I**.	**I** like turtles.
Use **he** for a male.	**Dad** reads about turtles. **He** reads about turtles.
Use **she** for a female.	**Mariana** sees real turtles. **She** sees real turtles.
Use **they** for more than one person.	**Lucy and José** see turtles. **They** see turtles.

Read a Sentence

Look at the noun. Which pronoun can take its place?

Amy draws a turtle.

Write a Sentence

What do you think about turtles? Write a sentence that starts with **I**. Read it to a partner.

Restate an Idea

Listen and sing.

Song ((MP3))

Change and Grow

Animals, animals
Change as they grow,
Change as they grow.
This is what I heard.
This is what I heard.
This is what I know.
This is what I know.

Insects, too, insects, too,
Change as they grow,
Change as they grow.
This is what I heard.
This is what I heard.
This is what I know.
This is what I know.

Tune: "Frère Jacques"

242

Key Words

See how the **insect** will **change** as it grows.

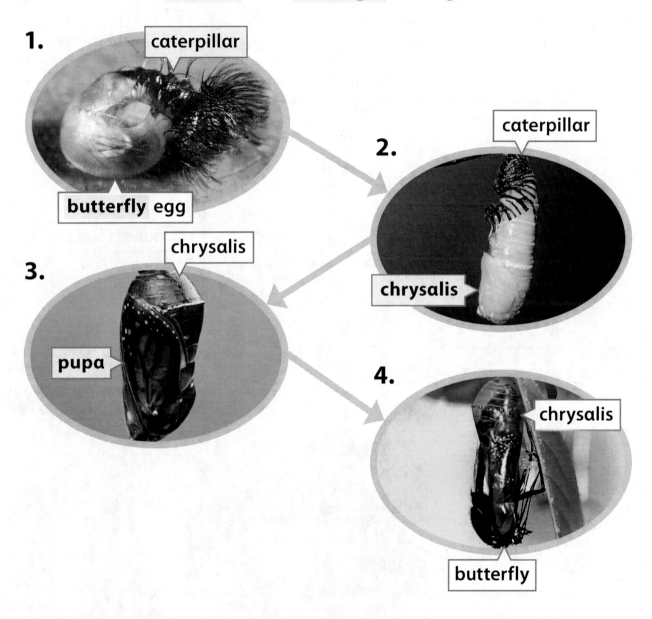

1. caterpillar
butterfly egg

2. caterpillar
chrysalis

3. chrysalis
pupa

4. chrysalis
butterfly

Talk Together

This insect changes as it grows. What do you know about how insects and animals change as they grow?

Identify Main Idea and Details

Main Idea and Details Chart

Main Idea:
Animals change as they grow.

> Write the main idea here.

Detail:
get bigger

Detail:
start moving

Detail:
change shape

> Write the details here.

Talk Together

Choose an animal. How does the animal **change** as it grows? Add the details to the chart.

More Key Words

attach

ring

You can **attach** keys to a ring.

born

This baby was **born** yesterday.

color

The **color** of the flower is red.

hard

The rock feels **hard**.

sequence

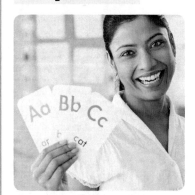

The letters are in order, or **sequence**.

Talk Together

Make word cards for each **Key Word**.

I was born in August.

Add words to My Vocabulary Notebook.
NGReach.com

Read a Science Article

A **science article** is nonfiction. It tells about things that are real.

✓ Look for diagrams.

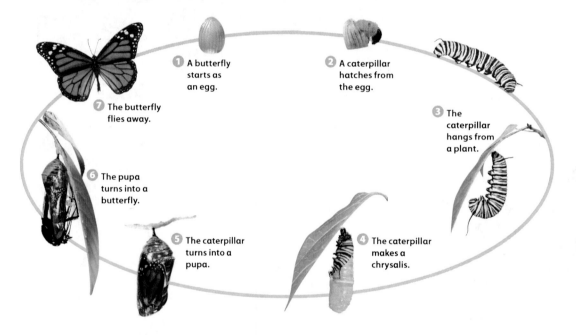

1. A butterfly starts as an egg.
2. A caterpillar hatches from the egg.
3. The caterpillar hangs from a plant.
4. The caterpillar makes a chrysalis.
5. The caterpillar turns into a pupa.
6. The pupa turns into a butterfly.
7. The butterfly flies away.

Diagrams show information.

Reading Strategy

As you read, **determine** importance.

What is the most important idea and why?

A Butterfly Is Born

by Fran Downey

butterfly

A **butterfly** sits on a plant.
She lays an egg.

egg

A butterfly egg is small.
It will hatch soon. Then
a **caterpillar** will come out.

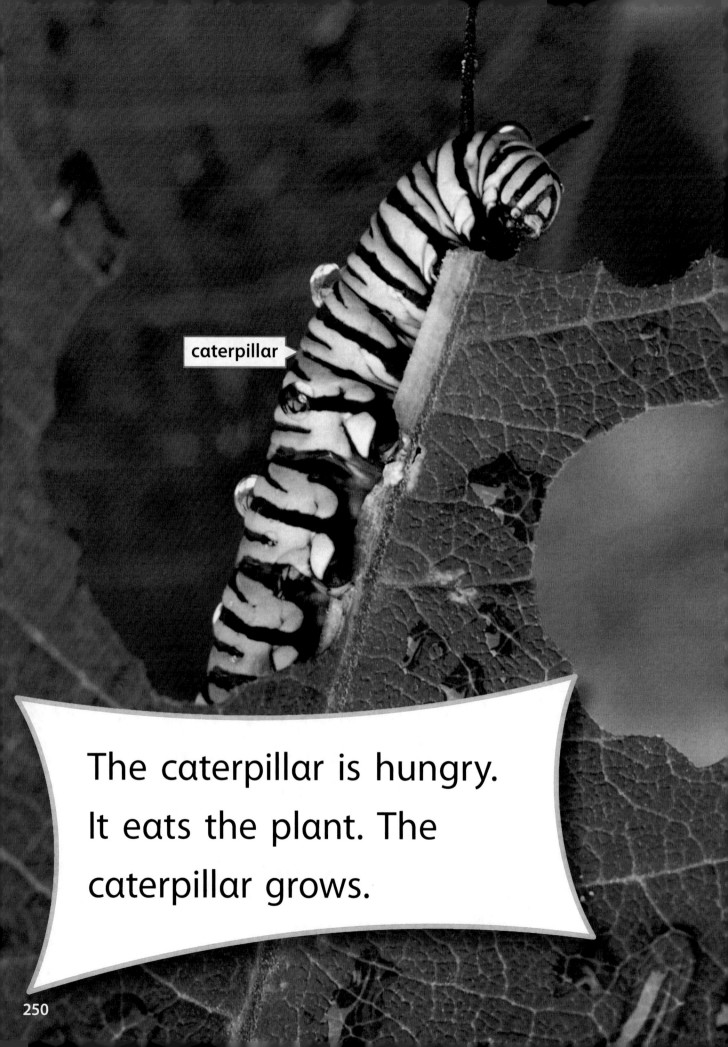

caterpillar

The caterpillar is hungry. It eats the plant. The caterpillar grows.

caterpillar

chrysalis

The caterpillar **changes**. It hangs from a plant. It makes a **chrysalis**.

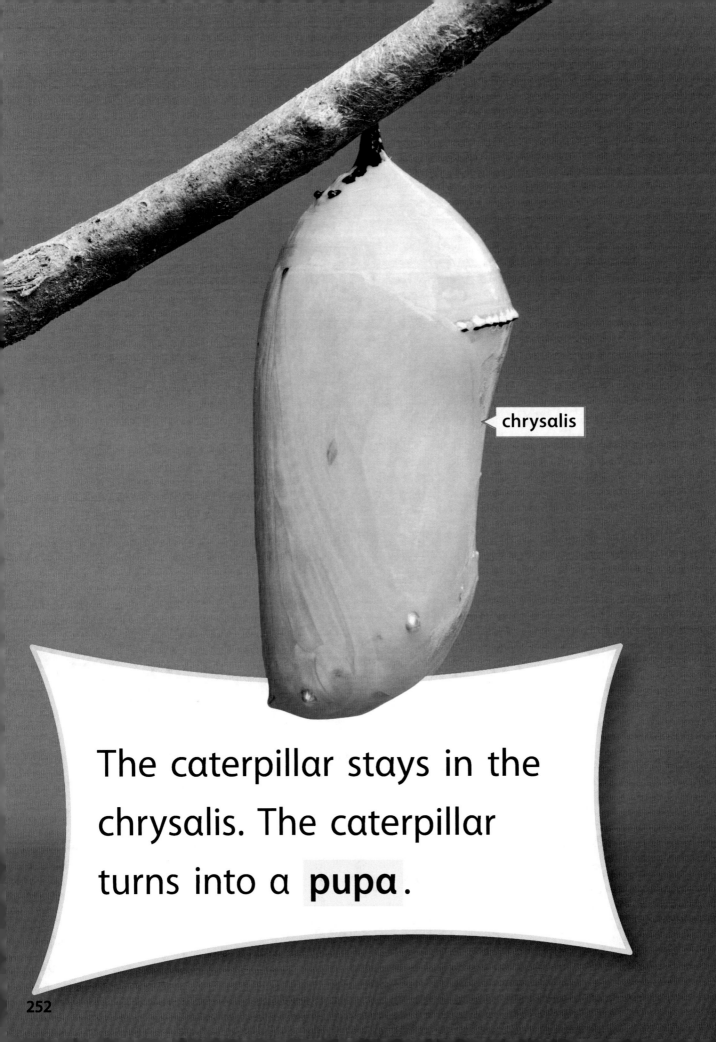

chrysalis

The caterpillar stays in the chrysalis. The caterpillar turns into a **pupa**.

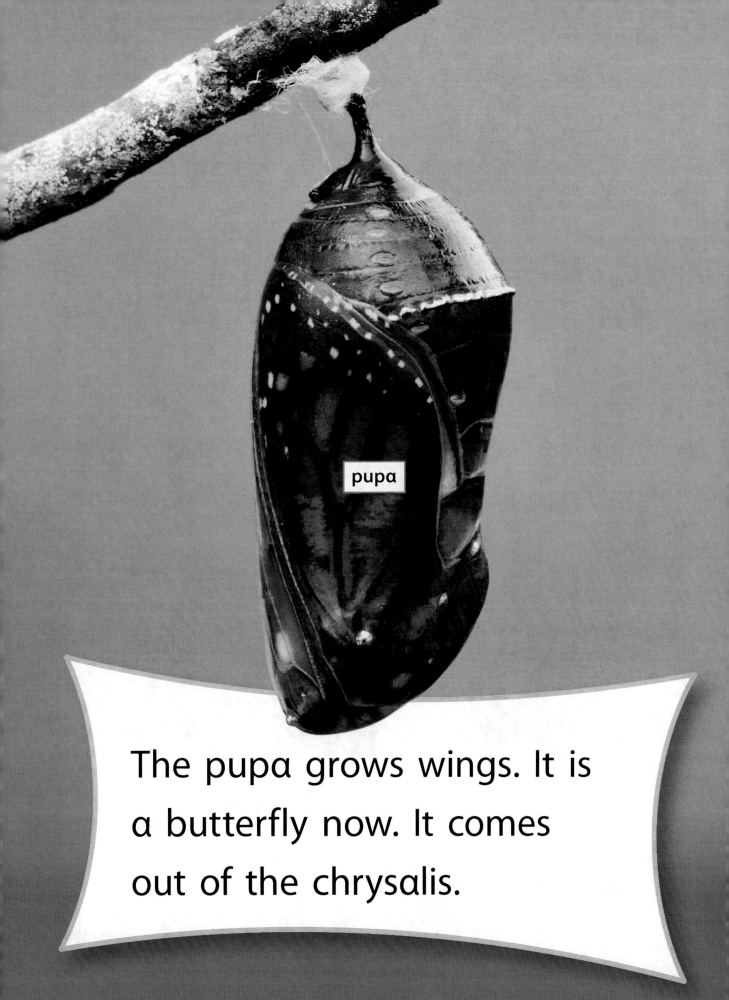

pupa

The pupa grows wings. It is a butterfly now. It comes out of the chrysalis.

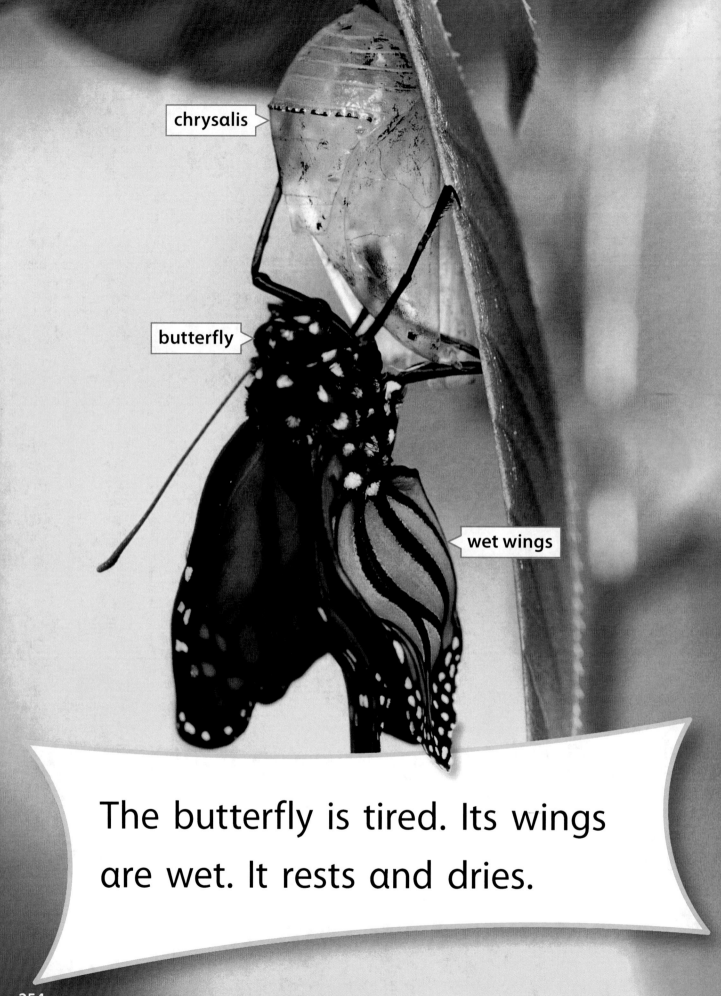

chrysalis

butterfly

wet wings

The butterfly is tired. Its wings are wet. It rests and dries.

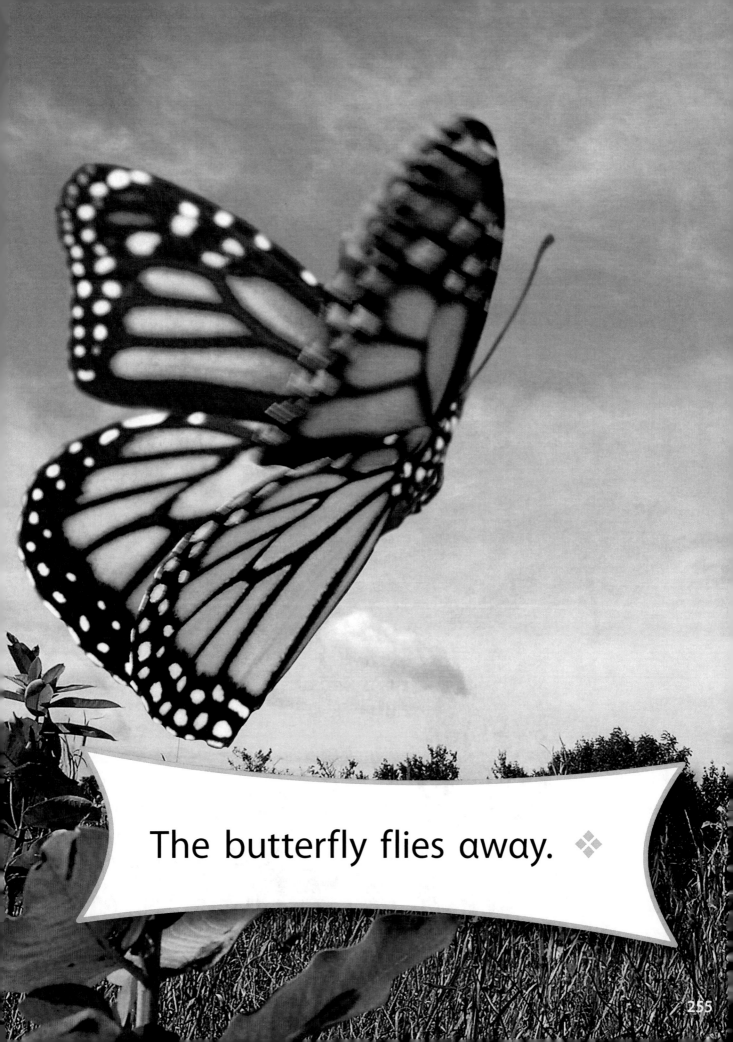

The butterfly flies away. ❖

A Butterfly Grows Up

1 A butterfly starts as an egg.

7 The butterfly flies away.

6 The pupa turns into a butterfly.

5 The caterpillar turns into a pupa.

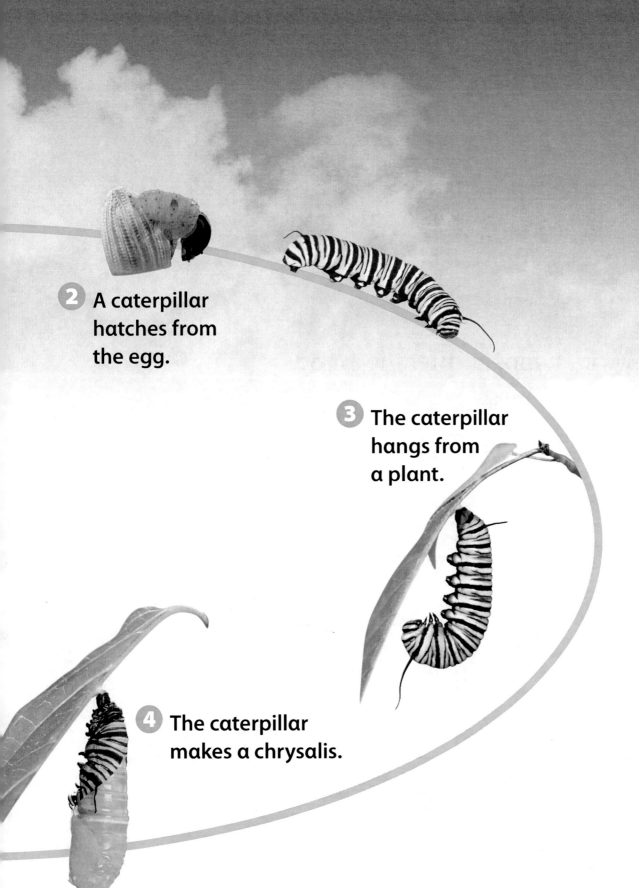

2 A caterpillar hatches from the egg.

3 The caterpillar hangs from a plant.

4 The caterpillar makes a chrysalis.

Talk About It

1. What is the size of a **butterfly** egg?

A butterfly egg is ____ .

2. What does the **caterpillar** make to hang from a leaf?

The caterpillar makes a ____ .

3. What happens after the **pupa** grows wings?

After the pupa grows wings, it ____ .

Learn test-taking strategies.
NGReach.com

Write About It

Write the steps of how a butterfly is born.

1. _____
2. _____
3. _____
4. _____

Identify Main Idea and Details

Where does a butterfly come from?

Main Idea and Details Chart

Main Idea:
A caterpillar changes into a butterfly.

Detail:hatches from an egg
Detail:
Detail:

Summarize what you learned about a butterfly's life. Use your main idea and details chart.

A caterpillar turns into a butterfly.

Use Context Clues

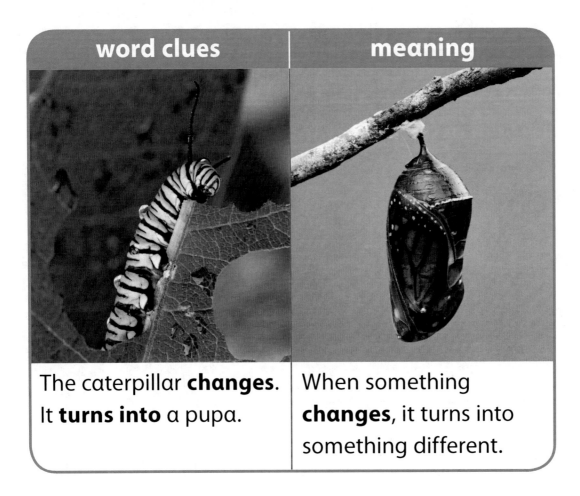

word clues	meaning
The caterpillar **changes**. It **turns into** a pupa.	When something **changes**, it turns into something different.

Look at the words and sentences around a new word. You might find **word clues** to figure out the meaning.

Try It Together

Look back at "A Butterfly Is Born." Find a sentence with the word **chrysalis**. Use word clues. Talk about the meaning of **chrysalis**.

260

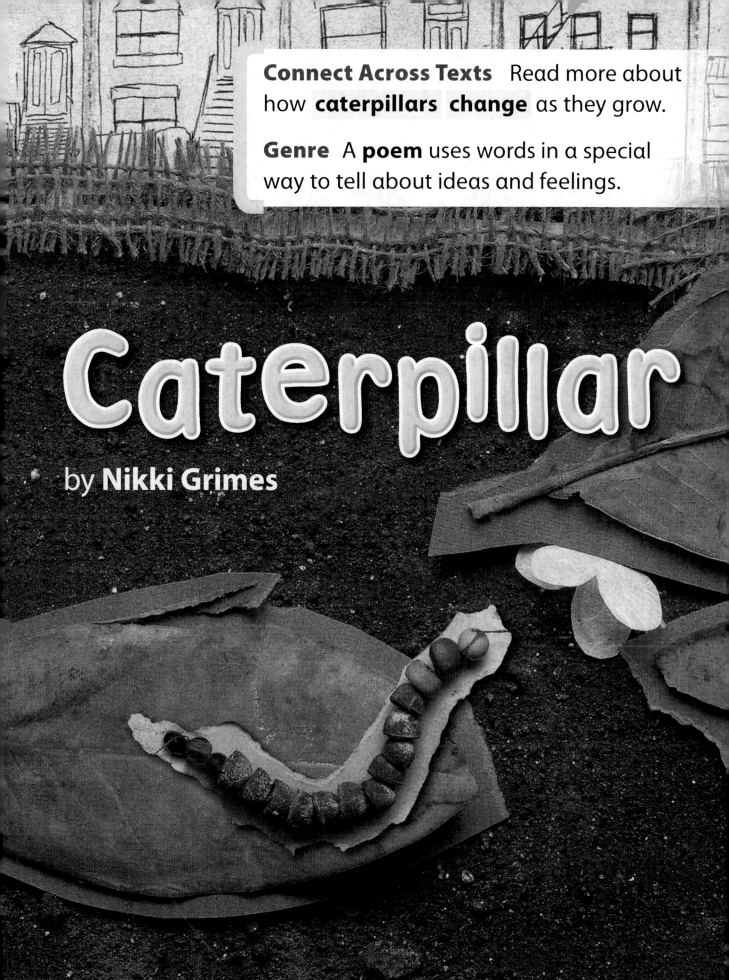

Connect Across Texts Read more about how **caterpillars** **change** as they grow.

Genre A **poem** uses words in a special way to tell about ideas and feelings.

Caterpillar

by **Nikki Grimes**

Caterpillar

The word wriggles in my pocket.
CATERPILLAR.
I reach for it, but it worms away
crawling as fast as it can. I get down
on my hands and knees to chase it.
Caterpillar, wait for me.
I haven't grown wings yet, either.
Soon, though!

Compare Genres

How is the information in "A Butterfly Is Born" and "Caterpillar" different?

Science Article

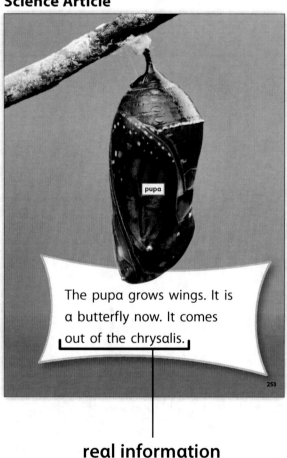

pupa

The pupa grows wings. It is a butterfly now. It comes out of the chrysalis.

253

real information

Poem

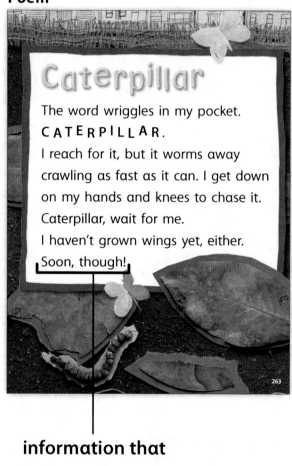

Caterpillar

The word wriggles in my pocket.
C A T E R P I L L A R .
I reach for it, but it worms away
crawling as fast as it can. I get down
on my hands and knees to chase it.
Caterpillar, wait for me.
I haven't grown wings yet, either.
Soon, though!

263

information that is not real

Talk Together

Think about what you read and learned. How do things change as they grow?

Possessive Words

A **possessive word** tells who owns or has something.

This is **Marshall's** caterpillar.

This is **his** caterpillar.

Grammar Rules **Possessive Words**

Use **her** for one girl or one woman.	♀	Butterflies land on **her** flowers.
Use **his** for one boy or one man.	♂	Dad will use **his** garden tools.

Read a Sentence

Does the sentence use the correct possessive word? How do you know?

Nikki looked for her caterpillar.

Write a Sentence

Write a sentence using a possessive word to tell what a friend brings to school.

Write Like a Storyteller

Write a Story

Have you heard stories about when you were younger? Tell one of your stories about growing up. Write the story for a friend.

Big Bike Time

by Jayan Ramahan

It was time for me to ride a big bike.

beginning ▷ **First**, I sat on the seat. Dad held the bike.

middle ▷ **Next**, I started to pedal. Dad held the bike.

end ▷ **Last**, I rode away. Dad watched me go!

Stories have a title and an author.

266

❶ Plan and Write

Language Frames

- First, I ____ .
- Next, I ____ .
- Last, I ____ .

Talk with a partner about stories you heard from your family. Pick one story. Tell your partner what happened first, next, and last.

Write your ideas. Then write the beginning, middle, and end of the story.

❷ Check Your Work

Revise and edit your writing. Use this checklist.

Checklist

- ☑ Can you repeat a word to make your story more fun to read?
- ☑ Check your sentences. Did you use a capital letter for the pronoun I?
- ☑ Read your story aloud. Check for words that sound alike. Correct spelling errors.

❸ Finish and Share

Finish your story. Write each sentence neatly. Leave spaces between words.

Read your story. Be a good listener.

I learned how to play soccer from my dad.

267

Share Your Ideas

Think about how animals change as they grow. Choose one of these ways to share your ideas about the **Big Question**.

Write It!

Draw a Sequence Chain

Draw a sequence chain that shows how an animal grows. Show three steps in the sequence. Number each step in order.

1. A turtle hatches.
2. It runs to the ocean.
3. It lays eggs.

Talk About It!

Question and Answer Game
Point to diagrams and photos in the unit. Ask **before and after** questions about sequence. Have your partner answer **before** or **after**.

Does Ruby fly **before** or **after** she is born?

After!

Do It!

Show the Order
Draw images of a caterpillar, a butterfly, and a pupa inside of a chrysalis. Give three students the drawings. Take turns putting the students in order to show how a caterpillar changes into a butterfly.

a
b
c
d
e
f
g
h
i
j
k
l
m
n
o
p
q
r
s
t
u
v
w
x
y
z

A

adult

*My dad is an **adult**.*

alive

plant

pot

*A plant is **alive**. A pot is not.*

attach

ring

key

*You can **attach** keys to a ring.*

B

baby

*The **baby** is sleeping.*

before

1   2   3

*One comes **before** two.*

born

*This baby was **born** yesterday.*

breathe

She likes to **breathe** the cold air.

bring

I **bring** my backpack with me.

bud

The flower **bud** will bloom in a few days.

business

My father owns a flower **business**.

butterfly

The **butterfly** used to be a caterpillar.

buy

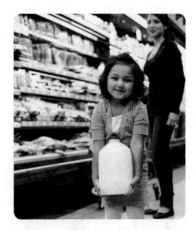

They **buy** milk at the store.

care

*I **care** for the plants.*

change

*The water will **change** into ice if you put it in the freezer.*

caterpillar

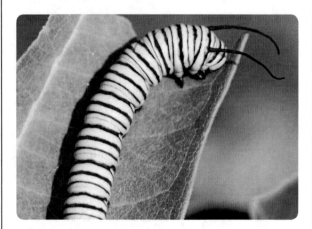

*This **caterpillar** is eating a leaf.*

chrysalis

*The caterpillar changes inside the **chrysalis**.*

celebrate

*Grandma **celebrates** her birthday.*

color

*The **color** of the flower is red.*

count

She **counts** how much money she saved.

D

delivery

Our mail **delivery** is late today.

drink

Orange juice is my favorite **drink**.

E

earn

The boy worked to **earn** money.

eat

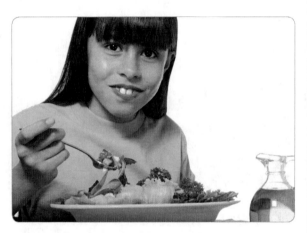

She **eats** all her salad!

egg

The chick is hatching from the **egg**.

a
b
c
d
e
f
g
h
i
j
k
l
m
n
o
p
q
r
s
t
u
v
w
x
y
z

energy

*Swimming takes a lot of **energy**.*

exercise

*My heart beats fast when I **exercise**.*

extended family

*This **extended family** is spending time together.*

factory

*This **factory** makes candy!*

family

*There are five people in my **family**.*

family member

*My uncle is a **family member**, but he does not live with us.*

flower

*This **flower** is a kind of daisy.*

food

*My family likes many kinds of **food**.*

form

*Chicks **form** inside of eggs until they are ready to hatch.*

fun

*Floating in the pool is **fun**!*

G

goods

milk

hammer

hat

*Stores sell these **goods**.*

group

*A **group** has more than two items.*

a b c d e f g h i j k l m n o p q r s t u v w x y z

grow

*If you give a plant plenty of water, it will **grow** bigger.*

hard

*The rock feels **hard**.*

hatch

*Snakes **hatch** out of eggs, much like birds do.*

health

*Brushing your teeth is good for your **health**.*

height

*This basketball player's **height** is seven feet.*

help

*I **help** fold the clothes.*

holiday

*Our favorite **holiday** is the Fourth of July!*

home

*Your **home** is where you live with your family. There are many different kinds of homes.*

idea

*Lori's **idea** is to go to the zoo.*

insect

*A ladybug is a type of **insect**.*

inside

*Books are **inside** this box.*

277

a b c d e f g h i **j** **k** **l** **m** n o p q r s t u v w x y z

J

job

My grandpa has a **job** at the grocery store.

light

The **light** is bright enough to read the book.

L

leaf

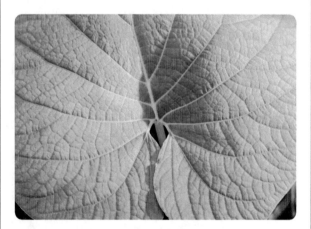

This **leaf** is bright green.

living

The goldfish is a **living** thing. The bowl is not.

length

The **length** of the carrot is 7 inches.

M

market

They are buying tomatoes at the **market**.

meal

*We eat our **meals** together.*

money

*He has a lot of **money**.*

move

*A sloth **moves** very slowly.*

needs

*Food and clothing are **needs**.*

neighborhood

*A parade came through our **neighborhood**.*

nest

*The bird is flying back to its **nest**.*

nonliving

Rocks and water are **nonliving** things.

P

parents

My **parents** like to cook with me.

petal

This flower has yellow and pink **petals**.

place

This school is a big **place**.

play

We **play** a game together.

project

I am so proud of my science fair **project**.

pupa

*This **pupa** will soon be an adult moth.*

ready

*The runner is **ready** to race.*

seed

*A tiny apple **seed**, can grow into a big apple tree!*

sell

*He **sells** flowers at the market.*

sequence

*The letters are in order, or **sequence**.*

service

*A **service** is work someone does for money, such as cutting hair.*

shape

*The **shape** of a ball is round.*

share

*We **share** the popcorn.*

ship

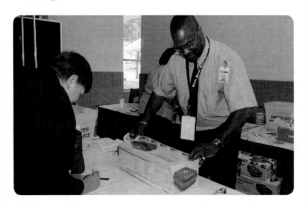

*He **ships** the present for my grandma.*

shop

*I like to **shop** at the bookstore.*

size

*My dad's shoes are not my **size**.*

special

*Today is her **special** day.*

store

*We are shopping at the **store**.*

sun

*The **sun** is very bright today.*

time

*Seven o'clock is the **time** we wake up.*

together

*We can win if we all work **together**.*

trip

*We take a **trip** in our car.*

visit

*I like it when my grandparents come for a **visit**.*

283

wants

Toys and games are **wants**.

worker

A **worker** at the restaurant makes lunch.

world

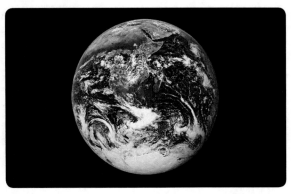

This is how our **world** looks from space.

Index

A

Academic vocabulary 7, 35, 71, 97, 137, 165, 205, 245

Activate prior knowledge 3, 67, 133, 201

Action verbs 156, **190**, 197

Adjectives 93, **127**, 129

Animal Life Cycles 200, 201, 202, 203, 207-229, 235-239, 240, 242, 243, 244, 246-257, 258, 259, 260, 261-263, 264, 268, 269
see also Butterflies, Caterpillars, Turtles

Arizona 57-59

Ask questions
about stories **138**, 154, **166, 269**
of others
see Speaking
types
literal 138, **162**, 163, 164, 166, 269

Author's purpose 160

Author's style 53, 117, 186, 231

B

Build Background 3, 67, 133, 201

Butterflies 246-257, 258, 259, 260

C

Categorizing 88, 120, 129, 199

Caterpillars 261-263, 264

Characters,
actions 53, 232
compare 232
feelings 232
story 53, 96, 119, 206

Clarifying meaning
See Plan and monitor

Compare
author's purpose **30, 160**
genres **60, 92, 126, 194, 240, 264**
texts 25, 57, 60, 89, 92, 121, 126, 157, 191, 194, 235, 240, 261, 264

Compare and contrast 88, 154, 164

Complete Sentences 22, 31, 54, 61, 86, 93, 118, 127, 154, 161, 195, 232, 241, 258, 265

Comprehension strategies
see Strategies for reading comprehension

Connections, making
text to own experiences 22, 30, 54, 86, 160, 194
text to text **25, 57,** 60, **89,** 92, **121,** 126, **157, 191,** 194, **235,** 240, **261,** 264
text to larger community 60

Content Vocabulary
see Vocabulary

Context clues
using to determine meanings **234**, **260**
unfamiliar words **234, 260**

Conventions, in writing
capitalization
for proper nouns 61, 63
for salutation and closing of letter 58, 197
parts of speech
adjectives 93, 127, 129
see also Adjectives
nouns 31, 61, 63, 93, 127
see also Nouns, Plural nouns, Proper nouns
pronouns 241, 267
see also Pronouns, Subject pronouns
verbs 161, 195, 197
see also Action verbs, Present tense verbs, Subject-verb agreement, Verbs
punctuation
see also Sentences

Creative projects 3, 24, 65, 67, 131, 133, 156, 199, 201, 233, 269

Critical thinking 22, 54, 86, 118, 154, 288, 232, 258

D

Describe
actions **4**, 5, 6, 22, 86, 118, 232
people and things 5, 6, **68**, 69, 86, 93, 129

Determine importance
main idea and details **206**, **246, 259**
summarize 259
Details, locating 117
identifying **164, 189, 244**
about stories **164, 189**
see also Determine importance

Directions, following written 62, 63, 128, 129, 196, 197, 266, 267

E

Explain 69, 120, 128, 129, 133, 196, 201, 203, 234, 243, 244, 260

Express feelings 63, 196, 197

Express ideas 120, 131, 190, 241

Express needs and wants **134**, 135, 154, 164, 194, **196**, 197, 198, 199

Express opinions 197, 241

F

Facts, locating 70, **87**, 191

  list 70, **87**, 191

  about stories 70, **87**, 191

Families 2, 3, 4, 5, 6, 8-21, **22**, 23, 25-29, 30, 31, 32, 33, 34, 37-52, 54, 57, 60, 61, 62, 63, 64, 65

Feelings

  see Express feelings, Speaking, express feelings

Fiction 36-53, 72-85, 98-117, 206-230

Flowers 157-159

G

Genres 60, 92, 126, **194, 240, 264**

  diagram **89**, 92

  fact sheet **191**, 194

  folk tale 98, 126

  how to make something 128

  magazine article **25**

  online article **157**

  photo book **8**

  photo essay 62

  poem 166, 188, 194, **261**, 264

  postcard 57, 60

  project notebook **121**, 126

  science article **235**, 240, 246, **264**

  social studies article **138**

  song **72**, 92

  story 36, 60, 206, 240

Give information 31, **32**, 33, 34, 54, **55**, 65, 67, 69, 70, 93, 118, 119, 120, 133, 135, 136, 137, 161, 188, 189, 190, 201, 203, 243, 244, 258, 259, 260, 269

Goods and services 137, 138-153, 157-159, 166-185, 191-193

  see also Flowers, Markets, Money

Graphic organizers

  beginning-middle-end chart 204, 233

  character-setting-plot chart **96, 119**

  chart 64

  checklist 70, 87

  idea web 6, 23, 164, 189

  main idea and details chart **244, 259**

  sequence chain 203, 268

  setting chart **34, 55**

  T chart 130, 136, 155, 198

Grammar

  see Adjectives, Conventions, Nouns, Plural nouns, Possessive words, Present-tense verbs, Pronouns, Subject-verb agreement, Verbs

H

High-frequency words 4, 7, 33, 68, 94, 134, 137, 162, 202, 205, 242

I

Ideas

see Express ideas, Speaking, express ideas

K

Key words

see Vocabulary

L

Language Functions

see Speaking, Listening

Listening

ask for and give information 5, 6, 23, 33, 65, 70, 87, 97, 118, 120, 155, 156, 163, 164, 188, 190, 233, 234, 243, 244, 258

collaborate with peers 30, 60, 61, 63, 65, 88, 92, 96, 120, 126, 129, 131, 136, 156, 160, 164, 165, 190, 194, 197, 234, 240, 244, 245, 260, 264, 267

comprehend spoken language 5, 6, 30, 33, 34, 61, 63, 65, 69, 70, 92, 93, 95, 96, 120, 126, 131, 135, 160, 161, 163, 189, 194, 203, 240, 241, 264, 269

monitor understanding of spoken language 70, 120, 131, 137, 163, 260, 269

to discussions 5, 6, 30, 33, 34, 61, 63, 65, 70, 92, 120, 126, 136, 160, 164, 194, 240, 260, 264

to instructions

following 5, 6, 7, 23, 30, 33, 34, 35, 60, 61, 63, 65, 69, 70, 87, 88, 92, 95, 96, 97, 118, 119, 120, 126, 131, 135, 136, 155, 156, 160, 163, 164, 165, 188, 189, 190, 194, 199, 204, 203, 233, 234, 240, 243, 244, 245, 258, 259, 260, 264, 269

to language structures 62, 129, 190, 197, 199, 241, 267

to media

audio tape

CD ROM

DVD

MP3 4, 33, 68, 94, 134, 162, 202, 242

video 3, 67, 133, 201

to messages 67

to speakers

asking questions 70

being attentive 5, 6, 7, 23, 30, 33, 34, 35, 61, 63, 65, 69, 70, 87, 88, 92, 95, 96, 97, 118, 119, 120, 126, 129, 131, 135, 136, 155, 156, 160, 163, 164, 165, 188, 189, 190, 194, 197, 199, 203, 204, 233, 234, 240, 243, 244, 245, 258, 259, 260, 264, 267, 269

making comments 67, 120, 131

to stories 95, 96, 266, 267

to vocabulary 5, 7, 33, 35, 69, 70, 71, 95, 97, 135, 137, 163, 165, 203, 205, 243, 245

Literary analysis
see Characters, Setting, Plot

Living and nonliving things **67**, 68, 69, 70, 72-85, **86**, 87, 88, **89**, 90-91, 92, 95, 126, 130

Logical order
see Sequence

M

Main idea and details 244, 259
see also Determine importance

Mapping
beginning-middle-end chart **204**
character-setting-plot chart **96**
checklist 70
idea web 6, 164
main idea and details chart 244
setting chart 34
T chart 136

Markets 134, **135**, 138-153, **154**, 155

Media, non-print 3, 4, 33, 67, 68, 94, 133, 134, 162, 201, 202, 242

Money 191-193

Monitor comprehension
see Plan and monitor

N

Needs and wants
see Express needs and wants, Speaking, express needs and wants

Nonfiction 8-21, 25-29, 57-59, 89-91, 121-125, 138-153, 157-159, 191-193, 235-239, 246-257, 261-263

Nonliving things
see Living and nonliving things

Nouns 24, **31**, **56**, **61**, 63, **93**, **127**, **241**
see also Conventions, Plural nouns, Proper nouns

O

Opinions
see Express opinions, Speaking, express opinions

Oral language
see Speaking, Listening

Organize Ideas 6, 23, 34, 55, 63, 64, 70, 87, 96, 119, 129, 130, 136, 155, 164, 189, 197, 198, 203, 204, 233, 244, 259, 267, 268

P

Plan and monitor
monitor and clarify 72, 98

Plot 96, 119, 131, 204

Plural nouns 31

Poetry 166-185
rhyme 166, 188, 199
rhythm

Possessive words 265

Predict **36**, 54

Present tense verbs 161

Preview **36**

Pronouns **241**, 267
see also Conventions, Subject pronouns

Proper nouns 61, 63

Purpose for reading
get information **8**, 22

Q

Questions
see Ask questions, Listening, Speaking, Vocabulary, Writing

R

Reading
comprehension
see Strategies for reading comprehension
decoding
base words 31, 161
shared reading 190
see also Retelling

Reading strategies
see Strategies for reading comprehension

Redwood trees 121-125

Restate an idea **242**, 243, 258

Retell 23, **94**, 95, 96, 189, 202, 203, 232, 233

S

Sentences
complete, *see Complete sentences*
subject-verb agreement in 195, 197
types of 154

Sequence 202, 203, 233, **245**, 266, 267, **268**, 269

Set a purpose 8, 22

Setting 34, **35**, **55**, 62, 96

Songs 4, 33, 68, **72**, 73-85, 94, 134, 162, 202, 242

Sorting **88**, **120**, 129, **199**

Speaking
adapt spoken language for purposes 199
ask and answer questions 3, 30, 60, 67, 69, 70, 97, 118, 120, 126, 133, 135, 136, **162**, 163, 164, 188, 194, 203, 234, 241, 244, 258, 259, 264, 269
ask for and give information 5, 6, 23, 33, 65, 70, 93, 97, 118, 119, 120, 131, 136, 155, 161, 163, 164, 188, 189, 190, 199, 234, 243, 244, 258, 259, 260, 269
collaborate with peers 30, 60, 61, 63, 65, 88, 92, 96, 120, 126, 129, 131, 136, 137, 156, 160, 164, 165, 190, 194, 197, 205, 234, 240, 244,

245, 260, 264, 267

describe **4,** 5, 6, 22, **68,** 69, 86, 93, 119

engage in conversations 88, 131, 136, 156, 234, 267

explain 69, 120, 129, 133, 201, 203, 234, 243, 244, 260

express feelings 63, 197

express ideas 120, 131, 190, 241

express needs and wants **134,** 135, 154, 164, 194, 199

express opinions 197, 241

give information 31, 32, 33, 34, 54, 55, 65, 67, 69, 70, 93, 118, 119, 120, 133, 135, 136, 137, 161, 188, 189, 190, 201, 203, 243, 244, 258, 259, 260, 269

give presentations 63, 67, 129, 131, 197, 201, 204, 267

identify objects, people, and places 67, 70, 88, 93, 96, 120, 133, 164, 201, 260

narrate 131, 267

participate in discussions 6, 23, 30, 33, 34, 54, 55, 60, 65, 88, 92, 96, 120, 126, 136, 155, 156, 160, 163, 164, 194, 234, 240, 264

provide suggestions 88, 96, 120, 136, 156, 190, 234, 260

restate an idea **242,** 243, 264

retell **94,** 95, 96, 189, **202,** 203, 204, 232, 233, 267

share ideas 30, 60, 63, 65, 88, 92, 95, 96, 120, 126, 129, 131, 133, 136, 156, 160, 164, 194, 234, 240,

241, 264

share information 31, **32,** 33, 34, 54, **55,** 65, 67, 69, 70, 118, 119, 120, 133, 135, 136, 137, 161, 164, 188, 189, 190, 199, 201, 203, 205, 243, 244, 258, 259, 260

   tell a story 131, 266, 267

   use a variety of grammatical structures 62, 129, 197, 267

   see also Vocabulary

Spelling

   base words with inflectional endings 31, 161

   high-frequency words 7, 137, 205

      see also High-frequency words

   using resources to check 63, 129, 197, 267

Story elements

   see Characters, Plot, Setting

Strategies for reading comprehension

   see Ask questions, Determine importance, Plan and monitor, Set a purpose

Subject-verb agreement 195, 197

   see also Verbs

Subject pronouns 241, 267

Summarize 259

   see Determine importance

T

Tell a story 131, 266, 267

  Text features (list all specific text features here)

  captions 62

  diagrams **246**, 256

  headings **138**, 140, 144, 148

  photos **8**, 10, 12, 13, 14, 15, 16, 17, 18, 19, 20-21

Topic

  and main idea 160

Transition words 202, 203, 233, 266, 267

Trees

  see Redwood trees

Turtles 235-239, 241

U

  Unfamiliar words

  see Context clues

V

Verbs **156**, **161**, **190**, **195**, 197

  see also Action verbs, Conventions, Present tense verbs, Subject-verb agreement

Visualize 93

Vocabulary

  academic 7, 35, 71, 97, 137, 165, 205, 245

high-frequency words 7, 137, 205

  see also High-frequency words

science 69, 70, 95, 203, 243

social studies 5, 33, 135, 163

strategies

ask questions 97

count syllables 35

discuss words 137

draw pictures 165

make word cards 245

use words in context 7, 71, 205

W

Word clues

  see Context clues

World 25-29

Writing

  paragraphs 57, 197, 267

  sentences

    complete 22, 31, 54, 61, 86, 93, 118, 127, 154, 161, 195, 232, 241, 258, 265

    compound 65

    simple 31, 61, 93, 118, 127, 154, 161, 195, 241, 258, 265

    see also Writing forms

Writing forms

how to make something **128**

photo essay **62**

poem 188

story **266**

thank you letter **196**

Writing models

diagram **89**, 92

fact sheet **191**, 194

folk tale 98, 126

how to make something 128

magazine article **25**

online article **157**

photo book **8**

photo essay 62

poem 166, 188, 194, **261**, 264

postcard **57**, 60

project notebook **121**, 126

science article **235**, 240, **246**, 264

social studies article **138**

song **72**, 92

story 36, 60, 206, 240, 266

thank you letter 196

Writing process

drafting 63, 129, 197, 267

editing 63, 129, 197, 267

revising 63, 129, 197, 267

prewrite

planning 63, 129, 197, 267

organizing 63, 129, 197, 267

publishing 63, 129, 197, 267

Index, continued

Index of Authors

Adamson, Heather 9

Block, Lily 89

Boron, Stefanie 157

Burns, Gabrielle 121

Dorros, Arthur 36, 53

Downey, Fran 247

Emmett, Jonathan 207, 231

Fuentes, Mariana 235

Grimes, Nikki 261

Kratky, Lada Josefa 99, 117

Langer, Heather 191

Mayer, Cassie 139

Salas, Laura Purdie 73

Suen, Anastasia 167, 186

Thome, Josh 25

Tong, Amy 57

Index of Illustrators

Harry, Rebecca 207

Newton, Vanessa 73

Wehrman, Vicki 99

Zahares, Wade 166, 187

Acknowledgments, continued

Text Credits

Unit One

Capstone Press: Excerpt from *Families in Many Cultures* by Heather Adamson. Copyright © by Capstone Press. Reprinted by permission of Capstone Press. All rights reserved.

HarperCollins Children's Books: Adaptation of *Papa and Me* by Arthur Dorros, illustrated by Rudy Gutierrez. Text copyright © 2008 by Arthur Dorros, illustrations © 2008 by Rudy Gutierrez. Reprinted by permission of HarperCollins Children's Books, a division of HarperCollins Publishers.

Unit Two

Picture Window Books: Excerpt from *Are You Living?* by Linda Purdie Salas. Copyright © 2009 by Picture Window Books. Reprinted by permission of Picture Window Books. All rights reserved.

Macmillan/McGraw Hill: "The Daisy" originally published as "La Margarita" by Lada Kratky. Copyright © 1993 by Macmillan. Reprinted by arrangement with Macmillan/McGraw Hill.

Unit Three

Capstone Global Library Limited: Excerpt from *Our Global Community: Markets* by Cassie Mayer. Copyright © 2007 by Heinemann Library. Reprinted under license from Capstone Global Library Limited. All rights reserved.

Anastasia Suen and Studio Goodwin Sturges: Excerpt from *Delivery* by Anastasia Suen, illustrated by Wade Zahares. Text copyright © 1999 by Anastasia Suen. Reprinted by permission of the author. Illustrations copyright © 1999 by Wade Zaharas. Reprinted by permission of Studio Goodwin Sturges on behalf of the artist.

Unit Four

Scholastic, Inc.: Adaptation of *Ruby in Her Time* by Jonathan Emmett, illustrated by Rebecca Harry. Text copyright © 2004 by Jonathan Emmett, illustrations © 2004 by Rebecca Harry. Reprinted by permission of Scholastic Inc.

Houghton Mifflin Harcourt: "Caterpillar," by Nikki Grimes, illustrated by Javaka Steptoe, from *A Pocketful of Poems*. Copyright © 2001 by Nikki Grimes. Illustrations © 2001 by Javaka Steptoe. Reprinted by permission of Clarion Books, an imprint of Houghton Mifflin Harcourt Publishing Company. All rights reserved.

NATIONAL GEOGRAPHIC SCHOOL PUBLISHING

National Geographic School Publishing gratefully acknowledges the contributions of the following National Geographic Explorers to our program and to our planet:

Josh Thorne, 2008 National Geographic Emerging Explorer
Michael Fay, National Geographic Explorer-in-Residence
Cid Simoes and Paola Segura, 2008 National Geographic Emerging Explorers
Mariana Fuentes, National Geographic Grantee
Greg Marshall, National Geographic Scientist
Tim Samaras, 2005 National Geographic Emerging Explorer
Constance Adams, 2005 National Geographic Emerging Explorer
Michael DiSpezio, National Geographic Presenter

Photographic Credits

iv (tc) Simon Marcus/Corbis. v (tl) Michael Christopher Brown/National Geographic Image Collection. vi (tl) Jeff Greenberg/Alamy Images. vii (tl) Stephen Frink Collection/Alamy Images. ix (tr) Simon Marcus/Corbis. 2-3 (bg) Dean Mitchell/Alamy Images. 3 (inset) Liz Garza Williams/Hampton-Brown/National Geographic School Publishing. 5 Photodisc/Getty Images. 6 Digital Vision/Getty Images. 7 (bl) Orange Line Media/Shutterstock. (br) Stockbyte/Getty Images. (tc) Corbis Super RF/Alamy Images. (tl) Alistair Berg/Digital Vision/Jupiterimages. (tr) Glenda Powers/iStockphoto. 8 (l) GoGo Images Corporation/Alamy Images. (r) Studio DL/Corbis. 8-9 (bg) David Young-Wolff/Alamy Images. 10 Sean Sprague/Sprague Photo Stock. 12 GoGo Images Corporation/Alamy Images. 13 Corbis Premium RF/Alamy Images. 14 Fancy/Alamy Images. 15 Studio DL/Corbis. 16 Marc Edwards/Peter Arnold, Inc. 17 Simon Marcus/Corbis. 18 Blend Images/Alamy Images. 19 Cliff Parnell/iStockphoto. 20-21 Corbis. 22 Monkey Business Images/Shutterstock. 23 Image Source/Jupiterimages. 24 David Young-Wolff/Alamy Images. 25 4Real. 26 (b) Aaron Huey/4Real. (t) 4Real. 27 (b) Penelopy Kalopisi-Kennedy/4Real. (t) Melahnie Moodie/4Real. 28 (l) Carolina for Kibera. 28-29 (bg) Photos.com/Jupiterimages. (c) 4Real. 29 (r) Melahnie Moodie/4Real. 30 (bg) Photos.com/Jupiterimages. (c) 4Real. (l) Marc Edwards/Peter Arnold, Inc. (r) Melahnie Moodie/4Real. 31 (bl) PhotoDisc/Getty Images. (blc) PhotoDisc/Getty Images. (br) RTimages/Shutterstock. (brc) RTimages/Shutterstock. (tl) PhotoDisc/Getty Images. (tr) RTimages/Shutterstock. 33 (b) Monkey Business Images/Shutterstock. (t) A. Ramey/PhotoEdit. 34 Purestock/Alamy Images. 35 (bl) Pixland/Jupiterimages. (br) Ronnie Kaufman/Blend Images/Jupiterimages. (tcl) iodrakon/Shutterstock. (tcr) lillisphotography/iStockphoto. (tl) C Squared Studios/Photodisc/Getty Images. (tr) Sarah Hadley/Alamy Images. 53 Alex Dorros. 55 MIXA/Alamy Images. 57 DigitalStock/Corbis. 58-59 (bg) DigitalStock/Corbis. 59 (inset) DigitalStock/Corbis. 60 DigitalStock/Corbis. 61 PhotoDisc/Getty Images. 62 (b) Ariel Skelley/Blend Images/Jupiterimages. (c) Alex Kotlov/iStockphoto. (t) Masterfile. 64 Dean Mitchell/Alamy Images. 65 rphotos/iStockphoto. 66-67 (bg) Aflo/Alamy Images. 67 (inset) Liz Garza Williams/Hampton-Brown/National Geographic School Publishing. 70 (b) Mike Flippo/Shutterstock. (t) Liz Garza Williams/Hampton-Brown/National Geographic School Publishing. 71 (bl) Christina Kennedy/Alamy Images. (br) Blend Images/Alamy Images. (tc) Comstock/Jupiterimages. (tl) Elena Butinova/Shutterstock. (tr) Juice/Jupiterimages. 87 (l) Liz Garza Williams/Hampton-Brown/National Geographic School Publishing. (r) Liz Garza Williams/Hampton-Brown/National Geographic School Publishing. 88 (bcr) Robert Pickett/Papilio/Alamy Images. (bl) PhotoDisc/Getty Images. (br) Michael Melford/National Geographic Image Collection. (cl) G.K. & Vikki Hart/Photodisc/Getty Images. (rcc) Photodisc/Getty Images. (tcr) MetaTools. (tl) SuperStock. (tr) Stockbyte/Getty Images. 89 MIXA/Alamy Images. 90 (b) PhotoDisc/Getty Images. (tl) Bold Stock/Unlisted Images. (tr) Creatas/Jupiterimages. 91 (b) ethylalkohol/Shutterstock. (tr) Daniel Valla FRPS/Alamy Images. 92 (b) PhotoDisc/Getty Images. (tl) Bold Stock/Unlisted Images. (tr) Creatas/Jupiterimages. 93 (b) Roman Sigaev/Shutterstock. (c) N.Minton/Shutterstock. (t) Creatas/Jupiterimages. 97 (bl) Corbis Premium RF/Alamy Images. (br) James Pauls/iStockphoto. (tcl) Stockbyte/Getty Images. (tcr) Getty Images. (tl) Julián Rovagnati/Shutterstock. (tr) markomatovic/Shutterstock. 117 Lada Kratky. 119 Liz Garza Williams/Hampton-

Brown/National Geographic School Publishing. 121 (bg) DigitalStock/Corbis. (inset) George Steinmetz/National Geographic Image Collection. 122 Michael Christopher Brown/National Geographic Image Collection. 123 Michael Nichols/National Geographic Image Collection. 124-125 (bg) James P. Blair/National Geographic Image Collection. 126 Michael Nichols/National Geographic Image Collection. 127 Whitechild/Shutterstock. 129 Liz Garza Williams/Hampton-Brown/National Geographic School Publishing. 130 Aflo/Alamy Images. 131 (b) Rick Holcomb/Hampton-Brown/National Geographic School Publishing. (t) Liz Garza Williams/Hampton-Brown/National Geographic School Publishing. 132-133 (bg) Andrjuss/Shutterstock. 133 (inset) Liz Garza Williams/Hampton-Brown/National Geographic School Publishing. 136 (bl) Jeffrey Coolidge/Getty Images. (blc) Ralph Wachler/Bon Appetit/Alamy Images. (br) Blend Images/Alamy Images. (brc) Patrick Byrd/Alamy Images. (tcl) Spirit/Corbis. (tl) David Young-Wolff/PhotoEdit. (tr) Glowimages/Getty Images. (trc) Steve Skjold/Alamy Images. 137 (bl) Monkey Business Images/Shutterstock. (br) Peter Hansen/Shutterstock. (tcb) Mackey Creations/Shutterstock. (tcr) Premier Edition Image Library/Superstock. (tcr) PhotoDisc/Getty Images. (tl) BlueMoon Stock/Alamy Images. (tr) Jeffrey Smith/iStockphoto. 138 (inset) DBURKE/Alamy Images. 138-139 (bg) Tibor Bognár/Corbis. 140 Blend Images/Alamy Images. 141 Jeremy Richards/Shutterstock. 142 Steve McCurry/National Geographic Image Collection. 143 The Image Bank/Gary John Norman/Getty Images. 144 PhotoDisc/Getty Images. 145 Jeff Greenberg/Alamy Images. 146 Medioimages/Photodisc/Getty Images. 147 Layne Kennedy/Corbis. 148 DBURKE/Alamy Images. 149 adam eastland/Alamy Images. 150 Sherri R. Camp/Shutterstock. 151 PhotoDisc/Getty Images. 152 Jon Arnold Images Ltd/Alamy Images. 153 Robert Frerck/Odyssey Productions, Chicago. 154 Jeff Greenberg/Alamy Images. 155 picturepartners/Shutterstock. 156 Alex Segre/Alamy Images. 157 waldhaeusl com/Bildagentur Waldhaeusl/age fotostock. 158 (b) Paulo Fridman/Corbis. (t) Victor Sanchez de Fuentes. 158-159 (bg) Ricardo Azoury/iStockphoto. 159 (b) Picture Contact/Alamy Images. (t) Stephen Shepherd/Alamy Images. 160 (bg) Ricardo Azoury/iStockphoto. (br) Paulo Fridman/Corbis. (l) Blend Images/Alamy Images. (tr) Victor Sanchez de Fuentes. 164 Digifoto Diamond/Alamy Images. 165 (bl) Steven Bushong/iStockphoto. (br) PhotoDisc/Getty Images. (tc) Corbis/Jupiterimages. (tl) Floresco Productions/Cultura/Jupiterimages. (tr) Brand X/Jupiterimages/Alamy Images. 186 Cecil Stringfellow/Anastasia Suen. 187 Wade Zahares. 188 manley620/iStockphoto. 189 Liz Garza Williams/Hampton-Brown/National Geographic School Publishing. 191 Purestock/Alamy Images. 192 (bcl) Artville. (bcr) Artville. (bg) Idamini/Alamy Images. (bl) Artville. (br) Artville. (tcl) Ilene MacDonald/Alamy Images. (tcr) Ilene MacDonald/Alamy Images. (tl) Artville. (tr) Ilene MacDonald/Alamy Images. 193 (bl) M. Dykstra/Shutterstock. (br) Arvind Balaraman/Shutterstock. (t) David Young-Wolff/PhotoEdit. 194 (bcl) Artville. (bcr) Artville. (bg) Idamini/Alamy Images. (bl) Artville. (br) Artville. (tcl) Ilene MacDonald/Alamy Images. (tcr) Ilene MacDonald/Alamy Images. (tl) Artville. (tr) Ilene MacDonald/Alamy. 196 PhotoDisc/Getty Images. 197 Liz Garza Williams/Hampton-Brown/National Geographic School Publishing. 198 Andrjuss/Shutterstock. 200-201 (bg) Philip Quirk/Photolibrary. 201 (inset) Liz Garza Williams/Hampton-Brown/National Geographic School Publishing. 205 (bl) Geoff Tipton/iStockphoto. (br) Lorraine Kourafas/Shutterstock. (tl) iStockphoto. (tr) Aflo/Jupiterimages. 233 Marilyn Nieves/iStockphoto. 235 Stephen Frink Collection/Alamy Images. 236 Joshua Cinner. 237 Matthew Maran/Nature Picture Library. 238 Moodboard/

Illustrator Credits

English Language Proficiency Standards (ELPS)
English Language Arts and Reading (ELAR) TEKS

UNIT 1	My Family	
2–3	**Unit Opener** **Share What You Know** **Build Background** **Video**	**ELPS** • **1.A.** use prior knowledge and experiences to understand meanings in English • **4.F.5** use visual and contextual support to develop background knowledge needed to comprehend increasingly challenging language **ELAR TEKS** • **G1.16.A.1** recognize different purposes of media (with adult assistance) • **G1.27.B.1** follow instructions that involve a short related sequence of actions
4	**Language** **Describe**	**ELPS** • **1.F.** use accessible language and learn new and essential language in the process • **2.E.3** use linguistic support to enhance and confirm understanding of increasingly complex and elaborated spoken language • **2.F.2** listen to and derive meaning from a variety of media to build and reinforce language attainment • **3.B.1** expand and internalize initial English vocabulary by learning and using high-frequency English words necessary for identifying and describing people, places, and objects • **3.H.2** describe with increasing specificity and detail as more English is acquired • **4.F.4** use visual and contextual support to develop grasp of language structures needed to comprehend increasingly challenging language

5, 7	**Social Studies**
	Vocabulary
	
	Academic Vocabulary
	    Key Words
	    Talk Together
		ELPS
		• **3.D.** speak using content area vocabulary in context to internalize new English words and build academic language proficiency
		• **4.F.3** use visual and contextual support to develop vocabulary needed to comprehend increasingly challenging language
		• **4.F 8, 9, 10** use support from peers and teachers to develop vocabulary, grasp of language structures, and background knowledge needed to comprehend increasingly challenging language
		
		ELAR TEKS
		• **G1.6.C.1** determine what words mean from how they are used in a sentence, either heard or read
		• **G1.28.A.2** share ideas about the topic under discussion, speaking clearly at an appropriate pace, using the conventions of language

6	**Thinking Map**
	    Organize Ideas
	    Talk Together
		ELPS
		• **2.E.1, 2** use visual and contextual support support to enhance and confirm understanding of increasingly complex and elaborated spoken language
		• **2.G.1** understand the general meaning of spoken language ranging from situations in which topics are familiar to unfamiliar
		• **2. G. 4** understand the main points of spoken language ranging from situations in which topics are familiar to unfamiliar
		• **2.G.7** understand the details of spoken language ranging from situations in which topics are familiar to unfamiliar
		• **2.I.5** demonstrate listening comprehension of increasingly complex spoken English by taking notes commensurate with content and grade-level needs.
		• **4.D.1** use prereading supports to enhance comprehension of written text
		• **4.G.4** demonstrate comprehension of increasingly complex English by taking notes
		
		ELAR TEKS
		• **G1.RC-1.F.1** make connections to own experiences

Families in Many Cultures		
8–21	**Genre:** Photo Book **Photos** **Reading Strategy: Set** **a Purpose**	**ELPS** • **4.I.1** demonstrate English comprehension by employing basic reading skills • **4.F.6** use support from peers and teachers to read grade-level appropriate content area text • **4.G.1** demonstrate comprehension of increasingly complex English by participating in shared reading **ELAR TEKS** • **G1.4.C.1** establish purpose for reading selected texts

UNIT 1	My Family, *continued*	
22	*Think and Respond* **Talk About It** **Write About It**	**ELPS** • **1.E.3, 4** internalize new academic language by using and reusing it in meaningful ways in speaking and writing activities that build concept and language attainment • **1.H** develop and expand repertoire of learning strategies • **3.D.2** speak using content area vocabulary in context to build academic language proficiency • **4.I.2** expand reading skills • **4.F.7** use support from peers and teachers to enhance and confirm understanding • **4.G.3** demonstrate comprehension of increasingly complex English by responding to questions • **4.K** demonstrate English comprehension and expand reading skills by employing analytical skills such as evaluating written information and performing critical analysis • **5.B.2** write using content-based grade-level vocabulary **ELAR TEKS** • **G1.4.C.1** establish purpose for reading selected texts • **G1.RC-1.A.1** establish purposes for reading selected texts based upon desired outcome to enhance comprehension
23	*Reread and Retell* **Organize Ideas**	**ELPS** • **2.I.2** demonstrate listening comprehension of increasingly complex spoken English by retelling or summarizing spoken messages • **3.B.2** expand and internalize initial vocabulary by retelling simple stories and basic information represented or supported by pictures • **4.I.2** expand reading skills • **4.F.8** use support from peers and teachers to develop vocabulary needed to comprehend increasingly challenging language **ELAR TEKS** • **G1.14.B.2** identify important details in text, heard or read
24	*Word Work* **Identify Nouns**	**ELPS** • **4.F.3** use visual and contextual support to develop vocabulary needed to comprehend increasingly challenging language **ELAR TEKS** • **G1.6.A.2** identify words that name persons (nouns)
30	*Respond and Extend* **Compare Author's Purpose** **Talk Together**	**ELPS** • **2.G.1** understand the general meaning of spoken language ranging from situations in which topics are familiar to unfamiliar • **4.K** demonstrate English comprehension and expand reading skills by employing analytical skills such as evaluating written information and performing critical analysis **ELAR TEKS** • **G1.13.A.2** explain the author's purpose in writing about the text
31	*Grammar and Spelling* **Plural Nouns**	**ELPS** • **3.B.1** expand and internalize English vocabulary by learning and using high-frequency English words necessary for identifying and describing people, places, and objects • **3.C.1** speak using a variety of grammatical structures with increasing accuracy and ease • **4.F.4** use visual and contextual support to develop grasp of language structures needed to comprehend increasingly challenging language • **5.C.2, 3** employ English spelling patterns and rules with increasing accuracy **ELAR TEKS** • **G1.20.A.2.ii** understand and use nouns (plural) in the context of reading, writing, and speaking • **G1.22.D.1** spell base words with inflectional endings
32	*Language* **Give Information**	**ELPS** • **1.F.** use accessible language and learn new and essential language in the process • **2.E.3** use linguistic support to enhance and confirm understanding of increasingly complex and elaborated spoken language • **2.F.2** listen to and derive meaning from a variety of media to build and reinforce language attainment • **3.F.2** give information ranging from concrete vocabulary to abstract and content-based vocabulary • **4.F.4** use visual and contextual support to develop grasp of language structures needed to comprehend increasingly challenging language

33, 35	*Social Studies Vocabulary* *Academic Vocabulary* **Key Words** **Talk Together**	**ELPS** • **2.G.1** understand the general meaning of spoken language ranging from situations in which topics are familiar to unfamiliar • **3.D.1** speak using content area vocabulary in context to internalize new English words • **3.F.2** give information ranging from concrete vocabulary to abstract and content-based vocabulary • **4.F.3** use visual and contextual support to develop vocabulary needed to comprehend increasingly challenging language • **4.F 8, 9, 10** use support from peers and teachers to develop vocabulary, grasp of language structures, and background knowledge needed to comprehend increasingly challenging language **ELAR TEKS** • **G1.6.C.1** determine what words mean from how they are used in a sentence, either heard or read • **G1.28.A.2** share ideas about the topic under discussion, speaking clearly at an appropriate pace, using the conventions of language
34	*Thinking Map* **Identify Setting** **Talk Together**	**ELPS** • **2.E.1, 2** use visual and contextual support support to enhance and confirm understanding of increasingly complex and elaborated spoken language • **2.G.3** understand the general meaning of spoken language ranging from situations in which contexts are familiar to unfamiliar • **2G.9** understand the details of spoken language ranging from situations in which contexts are familiar to unfamiliar • **2.I.5** demonstrate listening comprehension of increasingly complex spoken English by taking notes commensurate with content and grade-level needs • **3.F.2** give information ranging from concrete vocabulary to abstract and content-based vocabulary • **4.D.1** use prereading supports to enhance comprehension of written text • **4.G.4** demonstrate comprehension of increasingly complex English by taking notes

Papá and Me

36–37	**Genre:** Realistic Fiction **Setting** **Reading Strategy:** **Preview and Predict**	**ELPS** • **4.I.1** demonstrate English comprehension by employing basic reading skills • **4.F.6** use support from peers and teachers to read grade-level appropriate content area text • **4.G.1** demonstrate comprehension of increasingly complex English by participating in shared reading • **G1.RC-1.A.1** establish purposes for reading selected texts based upon desired outcome to enhance comprehension
54	*Think and Respond* **Talk About It** **Write About It**	**ELPS** • **1.E.3, 4** internalize new academic language by using and reusing it in meaningful ways in speaking and writing activities that build concept and language attainment • **1.H** develop and expand repertoire of learning strategies • **2.H.1** understand implicit ideas in increasingly complex spoken language commensurate with grade-level learning expectations • **3.D.2** speak using content area vocabulary in context to build academic language proficiency • **4.F.7** use support from peers and teachers to enhance and confirm understanding • **4.G.3** demonstrate comprehension of increasingly complex English by responding to questions • **4.K** demonstrate English comprehension and expand reading skills by employing analytical skills • **4.I.2** expand reading skills • **5.B.2** write using content-based grade-level vocabulary **ELAR TEKS** • **G1.4.A.1** confirm predictions about what will happen next in text by "reading the part that tells" • **G1.4.B.4** locate details about stories • **G1.RC-1.D.1** make inferences about text • **G1.RC-1.F.1** make connections to own experiences
55	*Reread and Summarize* **Identify Setting**	**ELPS** • **2.I.2** demonstrate listening comprehension of increasingly complex spoken English by retelling or summarizing spoken messages • **3.B.2** expand and internalize initial vocabulary by retelling simple stories and basic information represented or supported by pictures • **4.I.2** expand reading skills **ELAR TEKS** • **G1.4.B.4** locate details about stories
56	*Word Work* **Identify Nouns**	**ELPS** • **4.F.3** use visual and contextual support to develop vocabulary needed to comprehend increasingly challenging language **ELAR TEKS** • **G1.6.A.3** identify words that name places (nouns)

English Language Proficiency Standards (ELPS)
English Language Arts and Reading (ELAR) TEKS, *continued*

UNIT 1	My Family, *continued*	
60	**Respond and Extend** **Compare Genres** **Talk Together**	**ELPS** • **2.G.1** understand the general meaning of spoken language ranging from situations in which topics are familiar to unfamiliar • **4.K** demonstrate English comprehension and expand reading skills by employing analytical skills
61	**Grammar and Spelling** **Proper Nouns**	**ELPS** • **3.B.1** expand and internalize English vocabulary by learning and using high-frequency English words necessary for identifying and describing people, places, and objects • **3.C.1** speak using a variety of grammatical structures with increasing accuracy and ease • **4.F.4** use visual and contextual support to develop grasp of language structures needed to comprehend increasingly challenging language • **5.B.1** write using newly acquired basic vocabulary • **5.C.2, 3** employ English spelling patterns and rules with increasing accuracy **ELAR TEKS** • **G1.20.A.2.iv** understand and use nouns (proper) in the context of reading, writing, and speaking • **G1.21.B.2.iii** use basic capitalization for names of people
62–63	**Writing Project** **Write as a Family Member (Write a Photo Essay)** **Plan and Write**	**ELPS** • **1.G.** demonstrate an increasing ability to distinguish between, and knowledge of when to use, formal and informal English • **3.F.2** give information ranging from concrete vocabulary to abstract and content-based vocabulary **ELAR TEKS** • **G1.17.A.1** plan a first draft by generating ideas for writing • **G1.17.B.1** develop drafts by sequencing ideas through writing sentences
62–63	**Writing Project** **Write as a Family Member (Write a Photo Essay)** **Check Your Work**	**ELPS** • **5.C.1, 2** spell familiar English words and employ English spelling rules with increasing accuracy • **5.E.1** employ increasingly complex grammatical structures in content area writing **ELAR TEKS** • **G1.17.C.** revise drafts by adding or deleting a word, phrase, or sentence • **G1.17.D.** edit drafts for grammar, punctuation, and spelling using a teacher-developed rubric
62–63	**Writing Project** **Write as a Family Member (Write a Photo Essay)** **Finish and Share**	**ELPS** • **3.E.1** share information in cooperative learning interactions • **3.I.** adapt spoken language appropriately for formal and informal purposes **ELAR TEKS** • **G1.17.E** publish and share writing with others
64–65	**Unit Wrap** **Share Your Ideas**	**ELPS** • **2.I.4** demonstrate listening comprehension of increasingly complex spoken English by collaborating with peers commensurate with content and grade-level needs • **3.E.1** share information in cooperative learning interactions • **3.I** adapt spoken language appropriately for formal and informal purposes **ELAR TEKS** • **G1.28.A.1** share information about the topic under discussion, speaking clearly at an appropriate pace, using the conventions of language • **G1.28.A.2** share ideas about the topic under discussion, speaking clearly at an appropriate pace, using the conventions of language

66–67	Unit Opener	**ELPS**
	Share What You Know	• **1.A.** use prior knowledge and experiences to understand meanings in English
	Build Background	• **4.F.5** use visual and contextual support to develop background knowledge needed to comprehend increasingly challenging language
	Video	**ELAR TEKS**
		• **G1.16.A.1** recognize different purposes of media (with adult assistance)
		• **G1.27.B.1** follow instructions that involve a short related sequence of actions
68	Language	**ELPS**
	Describe	• **1.F.** use accessible language and learn new and essential language in the process
		• **2.E.3** use linguistic support to enhance and confirm understanding of increasingly complex and elaborated spoken language
		• **2.F.2** listen to and derive meaning from a variety of media to build and reinforce language attainment
		• **3.B.1** expand and internalize initial English vocabulary by learning and using high-frequency English words necessary for identifying and describing people, places, and objects
		• **3.H.2** describe with increasing specificity and detail as more English is acquired
		• **4.F.4** use visual and contextual support to develop grasp of language structures needed to comprehend increasingly challenging language
69, 71	Science Vocabulary	**ELPS**
	Academic Vocabulary	• **3.D.** speak using content area vocabulary in context to internalize new English words and build academic language proficiency
	Key Words	• **4.F.3** use visual and contextual support to develop vocabulary needed to comprehend increasingly challenging language
	Talk Together	• **4.F 8, 9, 10** use support from peers and teachers to develop vocabulary, grasp of language structures, and background knowledge needed to comprehend increasingly challenging language
		ELAR TEKS
		• **G1.6.C.1** determine what words mean from how they are used in a sentence, either heard or read
		• **G1.28.A.2** share ideas about the topic under discussion, speaking clearly at an appropriate pace, using the conventions of language
70	Thinking Map	**ELPS**
	List Facts	• **2.E.1, 2** use visual and contextual support support to enhance and confirm understanding of increasingly complex and elaborated spoken language
	Talk Together	• **2.G.1** understand the general meaning of spoken language ranging from situations in which topics are familiar to unfamiliar
		• **2.I.3** demonstrate listening comprehension of increasingly complex spoken English by responding to questions and requests
		• **4.D.1** use prereading supports to enhance comprehension of written text
72–85	Are You Living?	**ELAR TEKS**
	Genre: Song	• **4.I.1** demonstrate English comprehension by employing basic reading skills
	Rhyme	• **4.F.6** use support from peers and teachers to read grade-level appropriate content area text
	Reading Strategy:	• **4.G.1** demonstrate comprehension of increasingly complex English by participating in shared reading
	Monitor	• **G1.4.C.2** monitor comprehension, making corrections when that understanding breaks down
		• **G1.4.C.3** monitor comprehension, making adjustments when that understanding breaks down
		• **G1.8.A.2** respond to rhyme in poetry
86	Think and Respond	**ELPS**
	Talk About It	• **1.E.3, 4** internalize new academic language by using and reusing it in meaningful ways in speaking and writing activities that build concept and language attainment
	Write About It	• **1.H** develop and expand repertoire of learning strategies
		• **3.D.2** speak using content area vocabulary in context to build academic language proficiency
		• **4.I.2** expand reading skills
		• **4.F.7** use support from peers and teachers to enhance and confirm understanding
		• **4.G.3** demonstrate comprehension of increasingly complex English by responding to questions
		• **4.K** demonstrate English comprehension and expand reading skills by employing analytical skills such as evaluating written information and performing critical analysis
		• **5.B.2** write using content-based grade-level vocabulary
		ELAR TEKS
		• **G1.4.B.8** locate details about other texts

UNIT 2	Shoot for the Sun, *continued*	

87	Reread and Describe **List Facts**	**ELPS** • **3.H.2** describe with increasing specificity and detail as more English is acquired • **4.I.2** expand reading skills **ELAR TEKS** • **G1.14.B.1** identify important facts in text, heard or read
88	Word Work **Sort Words**	**ELPS** • **4.F.3** use visual and contextual support to develop vocabulary needed to comprehend increasingly challenging language **ELAR TEKS** • **G1.6.D.1** identify words [for sorting] into conceptual categories • **G1.6.D.2** sort words into conceptual categories
92	Respond and Extend **Compare Genres** **Talk Together**	**ELPS** • **2.G.1** understand the general meaning of spoken language ranging from situations in which topics are familiar to unfamiliar • **4.K** demonstrate English comprehension and expand reading skills by employing analytical skills such as evaluating written information and performing critical analysis
93	Grammar **Adjectives**	**ELPS** • **3.B.1** expand and internalize English vocabulary by learning and using high-frequency English words necessary for identifying and describing people, places, and objects • **4.F.4** use visual and contextual support to develop grasp of language structures needed to comprehend increasingly challenging language **ELAR TEKS** • **G1.20.A.3** understand and use adjectives in the context of reading, writing, and speaking
94	Language **Retell a Story**	**ELPS** • **1. F.** use accessible language and learn new and essential language in the process • **2.E.3** use linguistic support to enhance and confirm understanding of increasingly complex and elaborated spoken language • **2.F.2** listen to and derive meaning from a variety of media to build and reinforce language attainment • **3.B.2** expand and internalize initial English vocabulary by retelling simple stories and basic information represented or supported by pictures • **3.H.1** narrate with increasing specificity and detail as more English is acquired • **4.F.4** use visual and contextual support to develop grasp of language structures needed to comprehend increasingly challenging language
95, 97	Science Vocabulary Academic Vocabulary **Key Words** **Talk Together**	**ELPS** • **2.G.1** understand the general meaning of spoken language ranging from situations in which topics are familiar to unfamiliar • **3.D.1** speak using content area vocabulary in context to internalize new English words • **4.F.3** use visual and contextual support to develop vocabulary needed to comprehend increasingly challenging language • **4.F.8, 9, 10** use support from peers and teachers to develop vocabulary, grasp of language structures, and background knowledge needed to comprehend increasingly challenging language **ELAR TEKS** • **G1.6.C.1** determine what words mean from how they are used in a sentence, either heard or read • **G1.28.A.2** share ideas about the topic under discussion, speaking clearly at an appropriate pace, using the conventions of language
96	Thinking Map **Identify Plot** **Talk Together**	**ELPS** • **2.E.1, 2** use visual and contextual support support to enhance and confirm understanding of increasingly complex and elaborated spoken language • **2.G.7** understand the details of spoken language ranging from situations in which topics are familiar to unfamiliar • **2.I.1** demonstrate listening comprehension of increasingly complex spoken English by taking notes commensurate with content and grade-level needs • **3.H.1** narrate with increasing specificity and detail as more English is acquired • **4.D.1** use prereading supports to enhance comprehension of written text

The Daisy		
98–117	Genre: Folk Tale **Plot** **Reading Strategy:** **Monitor**	**ELPS** • **4.I.1** demonstrate English comprehension by employing basic reading skills • **4.F.6** use support from peers and teachers to read grade-level appropriate content area text • **4.G.1** demonstrate comprehension of increasingly complex English by participating in shared reading **ELAR TEKS** • **G1.4.C.2** monitor comprehension, making corrections when that understanding breaks down • **G1.4.C.3** monitor comprehension, making adjustments when that understanding breaks down

118	Think and Respond **Talk About It** **Write About It**	**ELPS** • **1.E.3, 4** internalize new academic language by using and reusing it in meaningful ways in speaking and writing activities that build concept and language attainment • **1.H** develop and expand repertoire of learning strategies • **3.D.2** speak using content area vocabulary in context to build academic language proficiency • **4.F.7** use support from peers and teachers to enhance and confirm understanding • **4.G.3** demonstrate comprehension of increasingly complex English by responding to questions • **4.K** demonstrate English comprehension and expand reading skills by employing analytical skills • **4.I.2** expand reading skills • **5.B.2** write using content-based grade-level vocabulary
119	Reread and Describe **Identify Plot**	**ELPS** • **3.H.2** describe with increasing specificity and detail as more English is acquired • **4.I.2** expand reading skills
120	Word Work **Sort Words**	**ELPS** • **4.F.3** use visual and contextual support to develop vocabulary needed to comprehend increasingly challenging language **ELAR TEKS** • **G1.6.D.1** identify words [for sorting] into conceptual categories • **G1.6.D.2** sort words into conceptual categories
126	Respond and Extend **Compare Genres** **Talk Together**	**ELPS** • **2.G.1** understand the general meaning of spoken language ranging from situations in which topics are familiar to unfamiliar • **4.K** demonstrate English comprehension and expand reading skills by employing analytical skills
127	Grammar **Adjectives**	**ELPS** • **3. B. 1** expand and internalize English vocabulary by learning and using high-frequency English words necessary for identifying and describing people, places, and objects • **4.F.4** use visual and contextual support to develop grasp of language structures needed to comprehend increasingly challenging language **ELAR TEKS** • **G1.20.A.3** understand and use adjectives in the context of reading, writing, and speaking
128– 129	Writing Project **Write as a Teacher (Write How to Make Something)** **Plan and Write**	**ELPS** • **1.G.** demonstrate an increasing ability to distinguish between, and knowledge of when to use, formal and informal English **ELAR TEKS** • **G1.17.A.1** plan a first draft by generating ideas for writing • **G1.17.B.1** develop drafts by sequencing ideas through writing sentences • **G1.19.A.1** write brief compositions about topics of interest to the student
128– 129	Writing Project **Write as a Teacher (Write How to Make Something)** **Check Your Work**	**ELPS** • **5.C.1, 2** spell familiar English words and employ English spelling rules with increasing accuracy • **5.E.1** employ increasingly complex grammatical structures in content area writing **ELAR TEKS** • **G1.17.C.** revise drafts by adding or deleting a word, phrase, or sentence • **G1.17.D.** edit drafts for grammar, punctuation, and spelling using a teacher-developed rubric
128– 129	Writing Project **Write as a Teacher (Write How to Make Something)** **Finish and Share**	**ELPS** • **3.E.1** share information in cooperative learning interactions • **3.I.** adapt spoken language appropriately for formal and informal purposes **ELAR TEKS** • **G1.17.E** publish and share writing with others
130– 131	Share Your Ideas	**ELPS** • **2.I. 4** demonstrate listening comprehension of increasingly complex spoken English by collaborating with peers commensurate with content and grade-level needs • **3.E.1** share information in cooperative learning interactions • **3.I** adapt spoken language appropriately for formal and informal purposes **ELAR TEKS** • **G1.28.A.1** share information about the topic under discussion, speaking clearly at an appropriate pace, using the conventions of language • **G1.28.A.2** share ideas about the topic under discussion, speaking clearly at an appropriate pace, using the conventions of language

UNIT 3	To Your Front Door	

132–133	*Unit Opener* **Share What You Know** **Build Background** **Video**	**ELPS** • **1.A.** use prior knowledge and experiences to understand meanings in English • **4.F.5** use visual and contextual support to develop background knowledge needed to comprehend increasingly challenging language **ELAR TEKS** • **G1.16.A.1** recognize different purposes of media (with adult assistance) • **G1.27.B.1** follow instructions that involve a short related sequence of actions
134	*Language* **Express Needs and** **Wants**	**ELPS** • **1.F.** use accessible language and learn new and essential language in the process • **2.E.3** use linguistic support to enhance and confirm understanding of increasingly complex and elaborated spoken language • **2.F.2** listen to and derive meaning from a variety of media to build and reinforce language attainment • **3.B.3** expand and internalize initial English vocabulary by learning and using routine language needed for classroom communication • **4.F.4** use visual and contextual support to develop grasp of language structures needed to comprehend increasingly challenging language
135, 137	*Social Studies* *Vocabulary* *Academic Vocabulary* **Key Words** **Talk Together**	**ELPS** • **3.D.** speak using content area vocabulary in context to internalize new English words and build academic language proficiency • **4.F.3** use visual and contextual support to develop vocabulary needed to comprehend increasingly challenging language • **4.F 8, 9, 10** use support from peers and teachers to develop vocabulary, grasp of language structures, and background knowledge needed to comprehend increasingly challenging language
136	*Thinking Map* **Categorize** **Talk Together**	**ELPS** • **2.E.1, 2** use visual and contextual support support to enhance and confirm understanding of increasingly complex and elaborated spoken language • **2.G.2** understand the general meaning of spoken language ranging from situations in which language is familiar to unfamiliar • **2.G.5** understand the main points of spoken language ranging from situations in which language is familiar to unfamiliar • **2.I.1** demonstrate listening comprehension of increasingly complex spoken English by following directions • **4.D.1** use prereading supports to enhance comprehension of written text

Markets		

| 138–153 | **Genre:** Social Studies
Article
Heading
Reading Strategy: Ask
Questions | **ELPS**
• **4.I.1** demonstratae English comprehension by employing basic reading skills
• **4.F.1** use support from peers and teachers to read grade-level appropriate content area text
• **4.G.1** demonstrate comprehension of increasingly complex English by participating in shared reading

ELAR TEKS
• **G1.4.B.5** ask relevant questions about other texts |
| 154 | *Think and Respond*
Talk About It
Write About It | **ELPS**
• **1.E.3, 4** internalize new academic language by using and reusing it in meaningful ways in speaking and writing activities that build concept and language attainment
• **1.H** develop and expand repertoire of learning strategies
• **2.H.1** understand implicit ideas in increasingly complex spoken language commensurate with grade-level learning expectations
• **3.D.2** speak using content area vocabulary in context to build academic language proficiency
• **4.I.2** expand reading skills
• **4.F.7** use support from peers and teachers to enhance and confirm understanding
• **4.G.3** demonstrate comprehension of increasingly complex English by responding to questions
• **4.K** demonstrate English comprehension and expand reading skills by employing analytical skills such as evaluating written information and performing critical analysis
• **5.B.2** write using content-based grade-level vocabulary

ELAR TEKS
• **G1.4.B.5** ask relevant questions about other texts
• **G1.14.B.1** identify important facts in text, heard or read
• **G1.RC-1.F.3** make connections to the larger community |

155	Reread and Retell	**ELPS**
	Categorize	• **2.I.2** demonstrate listening comprehension of increasingly complex spoken English by retelling or summarizing spoken messages
		• **3.B.2** expand and internalize initial vocabulary by retelling simple stories and basic information represented or supported by pictures
		• **4.I.2** expand reading skills
		ELAR TEKS
		• **G1.14.B.2** identify important details in text, heard or read
156	Word Work	**ELPS**
	Identify Verbs	• **4.F.3** use visual and contextual support to develop vocabulary needed to comprehend increasingly challenging language
		ELAR TEKS
		• **G1.6.A.1** identify words that name actions (verbs)
160	Respond and Extend	**ELPS**
	Compare Author's Purpose	• **2.G.1** understand the general meaning of spoken language ranging from situations in which topics are familiar to unfamiliar
	Talk Together	• **4.K** demonstrate English comprehension and expand reading skills by employing analytical skills such as evaluating written information and performing critical analysis
		ELAR TEKS
		• **G1.13.A.1** identify the topic [of] the text
		• **G1.13.A.2** explain the author's purpose in writing about the text
161	Grammar	**ELPS**
	Present Tense Verbs	• **3.C.1** speak using a variety of grammatical structures with increasing accuracy and ease
		ELAR TEKS
		• **G1.20.A.1.ii** understand and use verbs (present) in the context of reading, writing, and speaking
162	Language	**ELPS**
	Ask Questions	• **1. F.** use accessible language and learn new and essential language in the process
		• **2. E. 3** use linguistic support to enhance and confirm understanding of increasingly complex and elaborated spoken language
		• **2.F.2** listen to and derive meaning from a variety of media to build and reinforce language attainment
		• **3.F.1** ask [for] information ranging from concrete vocabulary to abstract and content-based vocabulary
		• **4.F.4** use visual and contextual support to develop grasp of language structures needed to comprehend increasingly challenging language
163, 165	Social Studies Vocabulary	**ELPS**
		• **2.G.1** understand the general meaning of spoken language ranging from situations in which topics are familiar to unfamiliar
	Academic Vocabulary	• **3.D.1** speak using content area vocabulary in context to internalize new English words
	Key Words	• **3.F.1** ask [for] information ranging from concrete vocabulary to abstract and content-based vocabulary
	Talk Together	• **4.F.3** use visual and contextual support to develop vocabulary needed to comprehend increasingly challenging language
		• **4.F 8, 9, 10** use support from peers and teachers to develop vocabulary, grasp of language structures, and background knowledge needed to comprehend increasingly challenging language
		ELAR TEKS
		• **G1.6.C.1** determine what words mean from how they are used in a sentence, either heard or read
		• **G1.14.C.2** retell the order of events in a text by referring to the illustrations
		• **G1.28.A.2** share ideas about the topic under discussion, speaking clearly at an appropriate pace, using the conventions of language
164	Thinking Map	**ELPS**
	Identify Details	• **2.E.1, 2** use visual and contextual support support to enhance and confirm understanding of increasingly complex and elaborated spoken language
	Talk Together	• **2.G.1** understand the general meaning of spoken language ranging from situations in which topics are familiar to unfamiliar
		• **2. G. 7** understand the details of spoken language ranging from situations in which topics are familiar to unfamiliar
		• **2.I.1** demonstrate listening comprehension of increasingly complex spoken English by following directions
		• **4.D.1** use prereading supports to enhance comprehension of written text

English Language Proficiency Standards (ELPS)
English Language Arts and Reading (ELAR) TEKS, *continued*

UNIT 3	**To Your Front Door,** *continued*	
Delivery		

166–187	**Genre:** Poem **Rhyming Text** **Reading Strategy: Ask Questions**	**ELPS** • **1.1** demonstrate English comprehension by employing basic reading skills • **4.F.6** use support from peers and teachers to read grade-level appropriate content area text • **4.G.1** demonstrate comprehension of increasing complex English by participating in shared reading **ELAR TEKS** • **G1.4.B.1** ask relevant questions about stories • **G1.8.A.2** respond to rhyme in poetry
188	*Think and Respond* **Talk About It** **Write About It**	**ELPS** • **1.E.3, 4** internalize new academic language by using and reusing it in meaningful ways in speaking and writing activities that build concept and language attainment • **1.H** develop and expand repertoire of learning strategies • **3.D.2** speak using content area vocabulary in context to build academic language proficiency • **4.F.7** use support from peers and teachers to enhance and confirm understanding • **4.G.3** demonstrate comprehension of increasingly complex English by responding to questions • **4.K** demonstrate English comprehension and expand reading skills by employing analytical skills • **4.I.2** expand reading skills • **5.B.2** write using content-based grade-level vocabulary **ELAR TEKS** • **G1.8.A.2** respond to rhyme in poetry • **G1.8.A.5** use rhyme in poetry
189	*Reread and Retell* **Identify Details**	**ELPS** • **2.I.2** demonstrate listening comprehension of increasingly complex spoken English by retelling or summarizing spoken messages • **3.B.2** expand and internalize initial vocabulary by retelling simple stories and basic information represented or supported by pictures • **4.I.2** expand reading skills
190	*Word Work* **Identify Verbs**	**ELPS** • **4.F.3** use visual and contextual support to develop vocabulary needed to comprehend increasingly challenging language **ELAR TEKS** • **G1.6.A.1** identify words that name actions (verbs)
194	*Respond and Extend* **Compare Genres** **Talk Together**	**ELPS** • **2.G.1** understand the general meaning of spoken language ranging from situations in which topics are familiar to unfamiliar • **4.K** demonstrate English comprehension and expand reading skills by employing analytical skills
195	*Grammar* **Subject-verb Agreement: be and have**	**ELPS** • **3.C.1** speak using a variety of grammatical structures with increasing accuracy and ease • **4.F.4** use visual and contextual support to develop grasp of language structures needed to comprehend increasingly challenging language **ELAR TEKS** • **G1.20.A.1.ii** understand and use verbs (present) in the context of reading, writing, and speaking • **G1.20.B.1** speak in complete sentences with correct subject-verb agreement
196–197	*Writing Project* **Write as a Family Member (Write a Thank you Letter)** **Plan and Write**	**ELPS** • **1.G.** demonstrate an increasing ability to distinguish between, and knowledge of when to use, formal and informal English • **5.B.1** write using newly acquired basic vocabulary **ELAR TEKS** • **G1.17.A.1** plan a first draft by generating ideas for writing • **G1.17.B.1** develop drafts by sequencing ideas through writing sentences • **G1.19.B.2** write short letters that put ideas in a logical sequence • **G1.19.B.3** [write short letters] using appropriate conventions
196–197	*Writing Project* **Write as a Family Member (Write a Thank you Letter)** **Check Your Work**	**ELPS** • **5.C.1, 2** spell familiar English words and employ English spelling rules with increasing accuracy • **5.D.1** edit writing for standard grammar and usage, including subject-verb agreement • **5.F.1** write using a variety of grade-level appropriate sentence lengths in increasingly accurate ways • **5.F.2** write using a variety of grade-appropriate sentence patterns in increasingly accurate ways **ELAR TEKS** • **G1.17.C.** revise drafts by adding or deleting a word, phrase, or sentence • **G1.17.D.** edit drafts for grammar, punctuation, and spelling using a teacher-developed rubric

196–197	*Writing Project* **Write as a Family Member (Write a Thank you Letter)** **Finish and Share**	**ELPS** • **3.E.1** share information in cooperative learning interactions • **3.I.** adapt spoken language appropriately for formal and informal purposes **ELAR TEKS** • **G1.17.E** publish and share writing with others
198–199	*Share Your Ideas*	**ELPS** • **2.I.4** demonstrate listening comprehension of increasingly complex spoken English by collaborating with peers commensurate with content and grade-level needs • **3.E.1** share information in cooperative learning interactions • **3.I** adapt spoken language appropriately for formal and informal purposes **ELAR TEKS** • **G1.8.A.2** respond to rhyme in poetry • **G1.8.A.5** use rhyme in poetry • **G1.28.A.1** share information about the topic under discussion, speaking clearly at an appropriate pace, using the conventions of language • **G1.28.A.2** share ideas about the topic under discussion, speaking clearly at an appropriate pace, using the conventions of language

UNIT 4	Growing and Changing	
200–201	**Unit Opener** **Share What You Know** **Build Background** **Video**	**ELPS** • **1.A.** use prior knowledge and experiences to understand meanings in English • **4.F.5** use visual and contextual support to develop background knowledge needed to comprehend increasingly challenging language **ELAR TEKS** • **G1.16.A.1** recognize different purposes of media (with adult assistance) • **G1.27.B.1** follow instructions that involve a short related sequence of actions
202, 205	**Language** **Retell a Story**	**ELPS** • **1.F** use accessible language and learn new and essential language in the process • **2.E.3** use linguistic support to enhance and confirm understanding of increasingly complex and elaborated spoken language • **2.F.2** listen to and derive meaning from a variety of media to build and reinforce language attainment • **3.B.2** expand and internalize initial English vocabulary by retelling simple stories and basic information represented or supported by pictures • **3.H.1** narrate with increasing specificity and detail as more English is acquired • **4.F.4** use visual and contextual support to develop grasp of language structures needed to comprehend increasingly challenging language
203	**Science Vocabulary** **Academic Vocabulary** **Key Words** **Talk Together**	**ELPS** • **3.D.** speak using content area vocabulary in context to internalize new English words and build academic language proficiency • **4.F.3** use visual and contextual support to develop vocabulary needed to comprehend increasingly challenging language • **4.F 8, 9, 10** use support from peers and teachers to develop vocabulary, grasp of language structures, and background knowledge needed to comprehend increasingly challenging language **ELAR TEKS** • **G1.6.C.1** determine what words mean from how they are used in a sentence, either heard or read • **G1.14.C.2** retell the order of events in a text by referring to the illustrations • **G1.20.A.7** understand and use time-order transition words in the context of reading, writing, and speaking • **G1.28.A.2** share ideas about the topic under discussion, speaking clearly at an appropriate pace, using the conventions of language
204	**Thinking Map** **Identify Plot** **Talk Together**	**ELPS** • **2.E.1, 2** use visual and contextual support support to enhance and confirm understanding of increasingly complex and elaborated spoken language • **2.G.3** understand the general meaning of spoken language ranging from situations in which contexts are familiar to unfamiliar • **2.I.1** demonstrate listening comprehension of increasingly complex spoken English by following directions • **3.B.2** expand and internalize initial English vocabulary by retelling simple stories and basic information represented or supported by pictures • **4.D.1** use prereading supports to enhance comprehension of written text **ELAR TEKS** • **G1.9.A.2** retell a story's beginning, middle, and end with attention to the sequence of events • **G1.RC-1.E.1** retell important events in stories in logical order
Ruby in Her Own Time		
206–231	**Genre:** Animal Fantasy **Reading Strategy:** **Determine** **Importance**	**ELPS** • **4.I.1** demonstrate English comprehension by employing basic reading skills • **4.F.6** use support from peers and teachers to read grade-level appropriate content area text • **4.G.1** demonstrate comprehension of increasingly complex English by participating in shared reading?

232	Think and Respond	**ELPS**
	Talk About It	• **1.E.3, 4** internalize new academic language by using and reusing it in meaningful ways in speaking and writing activities that build concept and language attainment
	Write About It	• **1.H** develop and expand repertoire of learning strategies
		• **2. H. 1** understand implicit ideas in increasingly complex spoken language commensurate with grade-level learning expectations
		• **3.D.2** speak using content area vocabulary in context to build academic language proficiency
		• **4.1.2** expand reading skills
		• **4.F.7** use support from peers and teachers to enhance and confirm understanding
		• **4.G.3** demonstrate comprehension of increasingly complex English by responding to questions
		• **4.K** demonstrate English comprehension and expand reading skills by employing analytical skills such as evaluating written information and performing critical analysis
		• **5.B.2** write using content-based grade-level vocabulary
		ELAR TEKS
		• **G1.4.B.4** locate details about stories
		• **G1.9.B.3** describe reasons for [characters'] feelings
233	Reread and Retell	**ELPS**
	Identify Plot	• **2.I.2** demonstrate listening comprehension of increasingly complex spoken English by retelling or summarizing spoken messages
		• **3.B.2** expand and internalize initial vocabulary by retelling simple stories and basic information represented or supported by pictures
		• **4.I..2** expand reading skills
		ELAR TEKS
		• **G1.9.A.2** retell a story's beginning, middle, and end with attention to the sequence of events
		• **G1.20.A.7** understand and use time-order transition words in the context of reading, writing, and speaking
		• **G1.RC-1.E.1** retell important events in stories in logical order
		• **G1.RC-1.E.2** act out important events in stories in logical order
234	Word Work	**ELPS**
	Use Context Clues	• **4.F.3** use visual and contextual support to develop vocabulary needed to comprehend increasingly challenging language
		ELAR TEKS
		• **G1.6.C.1** determine what words mean from how they are used in a sentence, either heard or read
240	Respond and Extend	**ELPS**
	Compare Genres	• **2.G.1** understand the general meaning of spoken language ranging from situations in which topics are familiar to unfamiliar
	Talk Together	• **4.K** demonstrate English comprehension and expand reading skills by employing analytical skills such as evaluating written information and performing critical analysis
241	Grammar	**ELPS**
	Subject Pronouns	• **3.C.1** speak using a variety of grammatical structures with increasing accuracy and ease
		• **4.F.4** use visual and contextual support to develop grasp of language structures needed to comprehend increasingly challenging language
		ELAR TEKS
		• **G1.20.A.6** understand and use pronouns in the context of reading, writing, and speaking
		• **G1.21.B.1.ii** recognize basic capitalization for the pronoun "I"
		• **G1.21.B.1.iii** recognize basic capitalization for names of people
		• **G1.21.B.2.ii** use basic capitalization for the pronoun "I"
242	Language	**ELPS**
	Restate an Idea	• **1.F.** use accessible language and learn new and essential language in the process
		• **2.E.3** use linguistic support to enhance and confirm understanding of increasingly complex and elaborated spoken language
		• **2.F.2** listen to and derive meaning from a variety of media to build and reinforce language attainment
		• **3.G.2** express ideas on a variety of social and grade-appropriate academic topics
		• **4.F.4** use visual and contextual support to develop grasp of language structures needed to comprehend increasingly challenging language

UNIT 4	**Growing and Changing,** *continued*	
243, 245	*Science Vocabulary* *Academic Vocabulary* **Key Words** **Talk Together**	**ELPS** • **2.G.1** understand the general meaning of spoken language ranging from situations in which topics are familiar to unfamiliar • **3.D.1** speak using content area vocabulary in context to internalize new English words • **4.F.3** use visual and contextual support to develop vocabulary needed to comprehend increasingly challenging language • **4.F 8, 9, 10** use support from peers and teachers to develop vocabulary, grasp of language structures, and background knowledge needed to comprehend increasingly challenging language **ELAR TEKS** • **G1.6.C.1** determine what words mean from how they are used in a sentence, either heard or read • **G1.28.A.2** share ideas about the topic under discussion, speaking clearly at an appropriate pace, using the conventions of language
244	*Thinking Map* **Identify Main Idea and Details** **Talk Together**	**ELPS** • **2.E.1, 2** use visual and contextual support support to enhance and confirm understanding of increasingly complex and elaborated spoken language • **2. G. 4** understand the main points of spoken language ranging from situations in which topics are familiar to unfamiliar • **2. G. 7** understand the details of spoken language ranging from situations in which topics are familiar to unfamiliar • **4.D.1** use prereading supports to enhance comprehension of written text • **4.G.4** demonstrate comprehension of increasingly complex English by taking notes

A Butterfly Is Born		
246– 257	**Genre:** Science Article **Reading Strategy:** **Determine** **Importance**	**ELPS** • **4.I.1** demonstrate English comprehension by employing basic reading skills • **4.F.1** use support from peers and teachers to read grade-level appropriate content area text • **4.G.1** demonstrate comprehension of increasingly complex English by participating in shared reading
258	*Think and Respond* **Talk About It** **Write About It**	**ELPS** • **1.E.3, 4** internalize new academic language by using and reusing it in meaningful ways in speaking and writing activities that build concept and language attainment • **1.H** develop and expand repertoire of learning strategies • **3.D.2** speak using content area vocabulary in context to build academic language proficiency • **4.F.7** use support from peers and teachers to enhance and confirm understanding • **4.G.3** demonstrate comprehension of increasingly complex English by responding to questions • **4.K** demonstrate English comprehension and expand reading skills by employing analytical skills • **4.I.2** expand reading skills • **5.B.2** write using content-based grade-level vocabulary **ELAR TEKS** • **G1.14.B.1** identify important facts in text, heard or read • **G1.14.B.2** identify important details in text, heard or read • **G1.14.C.1** retell the order of events in a text by referring to the words • **G1.14.C.2** retell the order of events in a text by referring to the illustrations
259	*Reread and Summarize* **Identify Main Idea and Details**	**ELPS** • **4.G.2** demonstrate comprehension of increasingly complex English by retelling or summarizing material • **4.I.2** expand reading skills **ELAR TEKS** • **G1.14.A.1** restate the main idea, heard or read • **G1.14.B.2** identify important details in text, heard or read
260	*Word Work* **Use Context Clues**	**ELPS** • **4.F.3** use visual and contextual support to develop vocabulary needed to comprehend increasingly challenging language **ELAR TEKS** • **G1.6.C.1** determine what words mean from how they are used in a sentence, either heard or read

264	**Respond and Extend** **Compare Genres** **Talk Together**	**ELPS** • **2.G.1** understand the general meaning of spoken language ranging from situations in which topics are familiar to unfamiliar • **4.K** demonstrate English comprehension and expand reading skills by employing analytical skills
265	**Grammar** **Possessive Words**	**ELPS** • **3.C.1** speak using a variety of grammatical structures with increasing accuracy and ease • **4.F.4** use visual and contextual support to develop grasp of language structures needed to comprehend increasingly challenging language **ELAR TEKS** • **G1.20.A.6** understand and use pronouns in the context of reading, writing, and speaking
266– 267	**Writing Project** **Write Like a Storyteller (Write a Story)** **Plan and Write**	**ELPS** • **1.G.** demonstrate an increasing ability to distinguish between, and knowledge of when to use, formal and informal English **ELAR TEKS** • **G1.17.A.1** plan a first draft by generating ideas for writing • **G1.17.B.1** develop drafts by sequencing ideas through writing sentences • **G1.18.A.1** write brief stories that include a beginning, middle, and end • **G1.20.A.7** understand and use time-order transition words in the context of reading, writing, and speaking
266– 267	**Writing Project** **Write Like a Storyteller (Write a Story)** **Check Your Work**	**ELPS** • **5.C.1, 2** spell familiar English words and employ English spelling rules with increasing accuracy • **5.D.2** edit writing for standard grammar and usage, including pronoun agreement • **5.F.2** write using a variety of grade-appropriate sentence patterns in increasingly accurate ways **ELAR TEKS** • **G1.17.C.** revise drafts by adding or deleting a word, phrase, or sentence • **G1.17.D.** edit drafts for grammar, punctuation, and spelling using a teacher-developed rubric
266– 267	**Writing Project** **Write Like a Storyteller (Write a Story)** **Finish and Share**	**ELPS** • **3.E.1** share information in cooperative learning interactions • **3.I.** adapt spoken language appropriately for formal and informal purposes **ELAR TEKS** • **G1.17.E** publish and share writing with others
268– 269	**Share Your Ideas**	**ELPS** • **2.I.3** demonstrate listening comprehension of increasingly complex spoken English by responding to questions and requests • **2.I.4** demonstrate listening comprehension of increasingly complex spoken English by collaborating with peers commensurate with content and grade-level needs • **3.E.1** share information in cooperative learning interactions • **3.I** adapt spoken language appropriately for formal and informal purposes **ELAR TEKS** • **G1.28.A.1** share information about the topic under discussion, speaking clearly at an appropriate pace, using the conventions of language • **G1.28.A.2** share ideas about the topic under discussion, speaking clearly at an appropriate pace, using the conventions of language

Content-Area TEKS

Grade 1, Volume 1, Content Standards

Unit 1 My Family

page 2 — Social Studies
- **SS.G1.14.A** describe ways that families meet basic human needs
- **SS.G1.14.B.i** describe similarities in ways families meet basic human needs
- **SS.G1.14.B.ii** describe differences in ways families meet basic human needs
- **SS.G1.15.A.i** describe various beliefs of families and explain their importance
- **SS.G1.15.A.ii** describe various customs of families and explain their importance
- **SS.G1.15.A.iii** describe various traditions of families and explain their importance

Unit 2 Shoot for the Sun

page 66 — Science
- **S.G1.9.A.i** sort and classify living things based upon whether or not they have basic needs
- **S.G1.9.A.ii** sort and classify living things based upon whether or not they produce offspring
- **S.G1.9.A.iii** sort and classify nonliving things based upon whether or not they have basic needs
- **S.G1.9.A.iv** sort and classify nonliving things based upon whether or not they have produce offspring
- **S.G1.10.B.i** identify the parts of plants
- **S.G1.10.B.ii** compare the parts of plants

Unit 3 To Your Front Door

page 132 — Social Studies and Math
- **SS.G1.7.A.iii** identify examples of goods in the community
- **SS.G1.7.A.vi** identify examples of services in the community
- **SS.G1.7.B.i** identify ways people exchange goods
- **SS.G1.7.B.ii** identify ways people exchange services
- **SS.G1.7.C.i** identify the role of markets in the exchange of goods
- **SS.G1.7.C.ii** identify the role of markets in the exchange of services
- **M.G1.1.C.i** identify individual coins by name
- **M.G1.1.C.ii** identify individual coins by value

Unit 4 Growing and Changing

page 200 — Science
- **S.G1.10.C** compare ways that young animals resemble their parents
- **S.G1.10.D.i** observe life cycles of animals
- **S.G1.10.D.ii** record life cycles of animals

For additional coverage of the English Language Proficiency Standards (ELPS) and Texas Essential Knowledge and Skills (TEKS), use these companion programs:

Reach into Phonics

**Grade 1
Literature Big Books**